This book is dedicated to my cousin Marie Flint and t
my friends Maurizio Eliseo and Paolo Piccione.

# Liners &
# Cruise Ships–2
## Some more notable smaller vessels

*by*
*Anthony Cooke*

Published by
## Carmania Press

Unit 202, Station House, 49 Greenwich High Road, London SE10 8JL, Great Britain.

© Anthony Cooke and Carmania Press
ISBN 0 9534291-5-6   First published 2000
British Library Cataloguing for Publication Data.
A Catalogue Record for this book is available from the British Library.

Artwork production by Alan Kittridge.
Printed by The Amadeus Press, Huddersfield, Yorkshire.

# Introduction

When *Liners & Cruise Ships: Some Notable Smaller Vessels* was published in 1996 it was something of a gamble. Would there be enough ship-lovers out there who were willing to buy a book which was not about the great and famous liners, but dealt instead with lesser-known passenger ships? Happily the book has sold well enough to justify a second volume. Once again, I have had the enjoyment of researching some fascinating ships and the satisfaction of introducing them to readers who might otherwise have hardly known them.

Ranging from the Australian *Bulolo* of 1938 to the Norwegian *Polarlys* of 1996, each ship in this new volume has an interesting story to tell. And there have been surprises. Who would have thought that Elder Dempster's plain and apparently rather dull *Accra* was such a successful ship, so well suited to the service to West Africa? Or that American Export's *Excalibur*, overshadowed by the famous and glamorous *Constitution* and *Independence*, carried her passengers in such comfort and style?

Of course, not all the stories told in this book are of success. There is the *Heraklion* (the former Bibby Line *Leicestershire*) whose loss in a terrible storm cost many lives and brought Typaldos Lines crashing down. And the unfortunate *Baudouinville*, plagued by innumerable mechanical problems, which, under many names and in many services, was almost always a failure.

Once again, I hope you will enjoy as much as I do rambling round the byways of passenger shipping history in the past sixty years.

Anthony Cooke
Greenwich
December, 1999

# Contents

# Acknowledgements

In writing a wide-ranging book, I have relied upon the generous help of many people who have shared their knowledge, recollections, photographs and brochures. I am very grateful to them all. In particular, I must thank those established authors who might have kept these resources to themselves for their own future use, but who have made them available for this book. They and the other helpful friends are listed below. If I have inadvertently omitted anyone, I apologise.

Bill Appleton; John Bamber of Gateway Transit Agencies Co.; Andrew Bell; Guillermo C. Berger of the Instituto de Estudios de la Marina Mercante Iberoamericana; Peter Browne; Marion Browning; Krzysztof Brzoza; Juan Eugenio Cañadas Bouzas; Louis Cochet; Luís Miguel Correia; Arthur Crook of Ashdown Marine, Ltd.; Gilles de Villers; Laurence Dunn, who as always helped me enormously; Father M. N. W. Edwards; Maurizio Eliseo; Mark Goldberg; Ambrose Greenway; Kevin Griffin of The Cruise People, Ltd.; Clive Harvey; Duncan Haws; John Henderson; Captain Bill Houghton-Boreham; Luís Filip Jardim; John Jedrlinic; Peter Knego; Mike Lennon; John Lingwood; John Macdonald; John and Jan McMichan; William H. Miller; Peter Newall; Peter Nicholson; James Nurse; Paul Pålsson; Paolo Piccione; Nicholas Pusenjak; Enrico Repetto; Theodore W. Scull; Glenn Smith; Donald Stoltenberg for the use of his splendid painting which can be seen on the rear cover of this book; Peter Telford; Rainer Tiemann; Marc Tragbar; Gordon Turner; Urbain Ureel; Admeto Verde; Bill Volum; Jenny Wraight of the Ministry of Defence Admiralty Library; Tony Winstanley; Victor Young; Charles Zuckerman.

Wherever possible I have sought information from primary sources, including Lloyd's Voyage Records; Lloyd's Casualty Reports; Lloyd's Register; and Admiralty Movements. Declan Barriskill at Guildhall Library has been particularly patient in coping with my requests.

Journals which have been helpful sources have included Lloyd's List; The Motor Ship; The Naval Architect; Sea Breezes; Shipbuilding & Shipping Record; Shipping Today & Yesterday; Ships Monthly; Steamboat Bill; The Times.

Books which have been consulted have been:

Bergenske, Byen Og Selskapet (Dag Bakka, Jr., Seagull Publishing, Bergen, 1993)
Berlitz Complete Guide To Cruising And Cruise Ships (Douglas Ward, Berlitz Publishing, New York, 1996, 1997, 1998)
Bibby Line, The, 1807-1990 (Nigel Watson, James & James, London, 1990)
Bibby Line: 175 Years Of Achievement (Edward Paget-Tomlinson, Bibby Line, Liverpool, 1982)
Century of North Sea Passenger Steamers, A (Ambrose Greenway, Ian Allan, Shepperton, 1986)
Cruise Ships, The (William H. Miller, Conway Maritime Press, London, 1988)
Dodero, Alberto, Su Vida, Su Obra, Su Barcos (Aurelio González Climent, Instituto de Estudios de la Marina Mercante Iberoamericana, Buenos Aires, 1989)
Donaldson Line (Peter Telford, World Ship Society, Kendal, 1989)
Glimpses (Sir Derek Bibby, Bibby Bros., Liverpool, 1991)
Historique de la Flotte des Messageries Maritimes (Commandant Lanfant, revised edition, Editions Hérault, Paris, 1997)
Merchant Fleets: 20. Elder Dempster Lines (Duncan Haws, TCL Publications, Hereford, 1990)
Navigator In The South Seas (Captain Brett Hilder, Seal Books, Adelaide, 1978)
Ocean Liner Odyssey (Theodore W. Scull, Carmania Press, London, 1998)
Paquetes Portugueses (Luís Miguel Correia, Ediçóes Inapa, Lisbon, 1992)
Prince Ships of Northern B. C. (Norman Hacking, Heritage House Publishing, Surrey, B. C. 1995)
St. Helena Lifeline (Ronnie Eriksen, Mallet & Bell Publications, Coltishall, 1994)
Sea Safari (Peter Kohler, P. M. Heaton Publishing, Abergavenny, 1995)
Significant Ships of 1996 (John Lingwood, The Royal Institution of Naval Architects, London, 1997)
South Atlantic Seaway (N. R. P. Bonsor, Brookside Publications, St. Brelade, Jersey, 1983)
Ulstein Info. No. 4 (Ulstein Group, Ulsteinvik, 1996)

# 1
# Bulolo

### Bulolo

Completed 1938. 6,267 gross tons. Length overall: 412 ft. 6 ins. Breadth: 58 ft. 2 ins. Draught: 25 ft. 3½ ins. Twin Screw. Diesel. Service Speed: 15 knots. Scrapped 1968.

Over the years, Burns, Philp & Co. Ltd. of Sydney (a trading house whose widespread interests around the South Pacific included much more than just shipping) owned a fleet ranging from island traders to well-known liners. They operated routes from Australia to the Pacific islands, to New Guinea, to Singapore and to Hong Kong. Without a doubt, the *Bulolo* was the most outstanding of their ships. The late 'thirties were a time when some very handsome ships were being built and the *Bulolo* was certainly one of them, very much in the then current motor liner style.

She was built by Barclay, Curle at their Whiteinch yard, Glasgow. They had already produced three successful small motor liners for Burns, Philp and so it was not surprising that the contract for the new ship went to them too. She was quite a sophisticated vessel with, for instance, very modern fire detection and sewage disposal systems. She was powered by two 6-cylinder diesel engines of the Burmeister & Wain - Harland & Wolff type which had been built by Kincaids of Greenock. There were five holds, served by 16 derricks and with a total capacity of about 170,000 cubic feet, including some insulated space. There were also tanks for carrying vegetable oils. Northwards, the ship would carry a wide variety of general cargo and on the return leg there might be quantities of copra (dried coconut) and other local produce.

As built, the *Bulolo* could carry 223 first class passengers and a further 16 in second class (i.e. better off non-whites - remember, this was 1938 and attitudes were different). The first class passengers travelled in some luxury. Lloyd's List described the public rooms as spacious and lofty, 'thus ensuring the maximum of light and air'. The *Bulolo*'s interior designers did not follow the lead set by Brian O'Rorke with the Orient Line's *Orion* three years earlier in devising a plain décor in light colours in order to give an air of coolness in hot climates. Instead, they retained the traditional wooden panelling, but in a typical modern late-1930s style. The dining saloon, for instance, was panelled in 'figured and burr ash with toned

**Looking very smart in her black and white livery, the *Bulolo* was a splendid motor liner and became very popular on the Australia – Papua New Guinea run.** *Laurence Dunn collection.*

**Lying next to the cargo liner *Clan Menzies*, the *Bulolo* is here being fitted out on the Clyde in 1938.**
*Laurence Dunn collection.*

sycamore and relief effected by the trim of walnut'. That room, incidentally, was air-conditioned while the rest of the passenger spaces relied on the then more usual punkah louvre system of ventilation.

Other public spaces included a music room with deep casements designed to catch the cool breeze created by the forward movement of the ship and leading out onto a small open deck overlooking the bow; a library; writing rooms; and a smoking room which gave onto a verandah deck. In addition there was a children's room. A swimming pool was also provided, with, as Andrew Bell was intrigued to notice, windows let into its sides. There were two de luxe cabins with private bathrooms; otherwise first class passengers were accommodated in 1-, 2-, 3- and 4-berth cabins without that luxury (but again, one has to remember that in 1938 standards were different). In addition to carrying first, and a few second, class passengers, the *Bulolo* could also accommodate native passengers in the after 'tweendecks.

The ship was launched on the 31st May, 1938 and ran her trials successfully on the Firth of Clyde that September, attaining a speed of 17 knots. Handed over to her owners, she left Glasgow on the 15th September and made her way to Middlesbrough to load coal. She left for Australia on the 20th September and arrived at Sydney on the 30th October. She entered service on what was the Australian equivalent of the old Empire routes of the British and other European powers. The territories of Papua and New Guinea were administered by Australia and the *Bulolo*'s passengers included officials, educationalists, missionaries and businessmen. The service was subsidised by the Australian government. It ran from Sydney to Brisbane, and then to a round of New Guinea ports - Port Moresby, Samarai, Madang, and Rabaul included. But the *Bulolo* made only eight of these round trips before events elsewhere overtook her.

There used to be a phrase, 'he had a good war,' - meaning that someone had done exceptionally well in the testing circumstances of war and had 'seen a lot of action'. One might say of the *Bulolo* that she, too, 'had a good war'. In September, 1939, with the Second World War only a few days old, she was requisitioned for the Royal Navy and sent to the Simonstown base in South Africa for conversion into an Armed Merchant Cruiser. She was fitted with seven 6-inch guns and two 3-inch.

In January, 1940 the conversion was complete and *HMS Bulolo*, pennant No. F82, was despatched to the West African port of Freetown for convoy escort duties, appearing in the Mersey in March – April, 1940 and on subsequent occasions at Belfast and in the Clyde. She was also used for raider patrols in the South Atlantic, captured two French merchant ships controlled by the pro-German Vichy government, stood by to evacuate Free French forces from West African ports (which proved to be unnecessary) and visited Tristan da Cunha. In this extraordinarily far-ranging phase of her naval career the *HMS Bulolo* also acted as a temporary troopship on the North Atlantic run but in 1942 she came to London for a second conversion, being refitted as a Landing Ship Headquarters by Silley Weir. The Allies were preparing to hit back and in the following months *HMS Bulolo* lay close inshore, acting as an operational headquarters during landings in North Africa, Sicily, mainland Italy (at Anzio) and Normandy. She also acted as a communications ship during the Casablanca conference between Winston Churchill and President Roosevelt in 1943. Churchill visited her before the D-Day landings and King George VI inspected the invasion fleet from her bridge. She did not remain unscathed during the fighting, being hit by a bomb. Four lives were lost, but although the ship was damaged she was able to continue her duties. In 1945 she was involved in the Malayan landings and she was at Singapore for the Japanese surrender. (This was commemorated by a Japanese sword displayed in a glass case in her entrance hall. Later it was on show in the Burns, Philp head office in Sydney.) She also carried refugees from Java. It was not until the 18th January, 1946 that the *Bulolo* started her return voyage to Britain from Bombay. Even now, she remained in government service, acting as an accommodation vessel at Rosneath on Gareloch on the Clyde.

Finally, late in 1946 she returned to the Barclay, Curle yard which she had left eight eventful years earlier. It took eighteen months to restore her to her pre-War state. She now had a passenger capacity of 219 in first class and 12 in second. On the 11th June, 1948 she sailed from Greenock for Liverpool where she was to pick up about

5

The *Bulolo* had an extremely active war and is seen here as *H.M.S. Bulolo*, a Landing Ship Headquarters, festooned with radio masts. *Peter Newall collection.*

200 passengers for Fremantle and Sydney, plus a cargo which included a quantity of motor cars. She finally arrived back at her home port of Sydney on the 24th July.

The *Bulolo* resumed her pre-War service to the New Guinea ports with her 18th August, 1948 sailing. Sydney to Sydney usually took something in the region of 30 days. Having survived so many wartime dangers, the ship very nearly succumbed after just three years of post-War service. As we have seen, one of her main cargoes was copra which old hands will tell you is not only likely to be bug-ridden but is also prone to fire. On the 29th August, 1951 the *Bulolo* was lying at her Sydney berth when fire was discovered in her No. 3 hold. There was a loud explosion and dense black smoke hindered the efforts of the firemen. Listing dangerously, the ship was towed stern-first into shallow water where she was flooded. However, by December she was repaired and back in service. In March, 1958 she was afire again. This time it was the result of arson with no less than seven separate fires having been set in the passenger quarters while she lay empty at Sydney. However, the blazes were extinguished quickly and damage was limited. Before that, in February, 1953, the *Bulolo* made an unsuccessful attempt to tow another Burns, Philp ship, the *Mangola*, off a coral reef on which she had stranded near the New Guinea coast. The *Bulolo* herself had several strandings over the years and also suffered long delays owing to strikes.

Despite these alarms, she maintained the passenger link with Papua New Guinea, together with the smaller *Malaita*, with some success and came to be regarded rather fondly by many Australians resident there. Bill

Volum travelled briefly on her in 1964 and describes her as 'a comfortable and well-appointed ship with much dark wooden panelling which by the 1960s seemed somewhat dated. The Burns, Philp ships were well-run. The company was by far the dominant trader in and to Papua and New Guinea during the years of the Australian administration. The ships were practically the only means of transport before the advent of the airlines and, to the end, were popular with tourists. Burns, Philp itself, having a near-monopoly of the trade in the area, tended to evoke mixed feelings among the expatriate Australians.' The master of the *Bulolo* at the time of Bill Volum's trip was Captain Brett Hilder, 'something of an identity in Burns, Philp and the fleet's senior master.' He was also the author of an autobiography, 'Navigator in the South Seas', which gives a fascinating insight into the operation of often quite small ships in an area where the veneer of civilisation was distinctly thin.

The *Bulolo* was only viable while she was subsidised. By the late 1960s, with air services well-established, the Australian government withdrew the subsidy, thus spelling her end. She was withdrawn in January, 1968 and on the 28th April she was towed out of Sydney harbour on her way to a shipbreaker's yard in Taiwan.

Burns, Philp continued in business until very recently, latterly largely as a food ingredients manufacturer in several parts of the World. They did still retain some shipping interests in the Papua New Guinea area, however. As for the *Bulolo*, she is commemorated, I gather, by a fine model which can be seen in the Australian National Maritime Museum at Sydney.

# 2

# Excalibur

***USN Dutchess / Excalibur / Oriental Jade.***
Completed 1944 as *USN Dutchess*, attack-transport. Converted into passenger/cargo liner *Excalibur*, 1948. 9,644 gross tons. Length overall: 473 ft. 1 ins. Breadth: 66 ft. 2 ins. Draught: 27 ft. 9³/₄ ins. Single screw. Geared turbine. Service speed: 16¹/₂ knots. Became *Oriental Jade* (1965). Scrapped, 1974.

Mention the name American Export Lines to a passenger ship enthusiast and he (or she) will immediately think of the *Independence* and the *Constitution*, two 23,000-tonners which seemed to epitomise the sleekness which set American liners apart from their rivals in the 'forties and 'fifties. But the company had other passenger ships - in particular the 'Four-Aces' which were in some ways a dry run for their slightly later and more famous fleetmates.

The *Excalibur*, *Exochorda*, *Exeter* and *Excambion* were the successors to a pre-War quartet with the same names which had also been advertised as the 'Four Aces'. Those pre-War ships were 9,000-ton combination passenger and cargo liners with notably good accommodation for 100 first class travellers. They established the company,

previously mainly a cargo line, as a quite significant competitor in the passenger trade between New York and the Mediterranean. Three of them were lost during the War and the fourth was sold to the Turks, so that replacement was a matter of some urgency at the end of hostilities.

As it happened, the opportunity lay close at hand. In the late 'thirties the company had started to introduce what was to be a large group of fast new 7,000-ton freighters, initially known as the 'Exporter' class. A few years later, with America at war, the U.S. government took delivery of a number of the ships which had originally been ordered by the company. In 1947, they were finally made available to American Export who decided to convert four of them into replacements for the 'Four Aces'. They were to perpetuate the names of their predecessors and the *USN Dutchess* (note, not *Duchess* - she was named after a county in the State of New York) therefore became the *Excalibur*.

Some companies give their ships a style which is instantly recognisable - the Danish company DFDS, for instance, in the post-War years and Swedish American. So it was with the ships designed for American Export,

*Excalibur*, **with her characteristic American Export Lines profile, was one of four sisters which maintained a passenger-cargo service between New York, seen here, and the Eastern Mediterranean.** *Laurence Dunn collection.*

Harbor, Manila and elsewhere. She also sailed around the Philippines re-deploying troops. Then, on the 7th October she arrived in Japan and landed occupation forces on several occasions. More happily, in November she was assigned to 'Magic Carpet' duty, carrying homeward-bound servicemen on voyages from Manila to San Francisco. Finally, on the 1st February, 1946 she left for the Atlantic coast, for Norfolk, Virginia where on the 4th April she was decommissioned and quickly handed over to the War Shipping Administration for disposal.

Between 1946 and 1948, fifteen 'Exporter'-class ships passed into the hands of American Export Lines, either directly owned or under charter from the United States Department of Commerce. The ones which were chosen to become the new 'Four Aces' were the *Dutchess*, the *Dauphin*, the *Queens* and the *Shelby*. The *Dutchess* was taken to the Brooklyn yard of Bethlehem Steel and stripped down more or less to the hull. Her steam turbines, which had been built at Bethlehem's Quincy, Massachusetts facility and which consisted of a high-pressure and a low-pressure unit double-reduction geared to a single screw, were retained. (American shipbuilders and owners were, on the whole, remarkably unenthusiastic about using diesel engines in large vessels.) It is interesting to read in the shipping journals of the day that the conversion of the ships was a long-drawn-out business owing to delays in the delivery of materials and to strikes - these were evidently not problems confined to war-stricken Europe.

When she emerged from the yard and ran her trials in September, 1948, the *Excalibur*, the first of the quartet, proved to be a very distinctive-looking ship, a pleasing mixture of the ultra-modern and the traditional. At first, the black paint of the hull was carried up to promenade deck level, but after a short time all four ships were given a white strake at main deck level which looked much neater and emphasised the pleasant sheer of the hull. The tall and unusually shaped funnel carried the line's colours - black with a thick white band, edged with red and bearing the large blue letter E. The 'Four Aces' continued to carry these colours even though the *Independence* and *Constitution* were given buff funnels with a blue top and plain white band edged in red. It was only in the early 'sixties that the two remaining 'Aces' fell into line.

The ships were quite big cargo-carriers with six holds, including a certain amount of refrigerated space. But it was the quarters for 125 all-first class passengers which

whether freighters or passenger liners. When almost everyone else had switched to the cruiser stern, the company remained loyal to the graceful old counter stern. But everything else was ultra-modern - particularly in the later ships, with their domed, slightly conical funnels and their rounded superstructure with those characteristic horizontal glazing bars in the windows. Internally, too, they had the spare sleekness so typical of the passenger spaces in American liners in the 'forties and 'fifties.

The ship which eventually became the *Excalibur* was laid down at the Bethlehem Steel yard at Sparrows Point in Maryland. It has been stated that if she had been built as an American Export freighter she would have been called *Executor*. As it was, when she was launched on the 26th August, 1944 she was named *Dutchess*. Ready by the beginning of November, she was commissioned by the U.S. Navy on the 4th. She and six of her sisters were completed as Attack Transports, intended to carry men and materials to invasion beaches where they would be landed by the ships' own craft. I have heard it suggested that they were particularly intended for the invasion of Japan. In the event, of course, the dropping of the atomic bomb and the surrender which followed made an invasion unnecessary.

The following account of the *Dutchess*'s naval career is based on information provided by John Jedrlinic. From December, 1944 to the end of February, 1945 she lay at Newport, Rhode Island, serving as a schoolship for precommissioning crews. She then moved to the Pacific, reaching Pearl Harbor on the 19th March where she undertook training exercises. Afterwards, she sailed for Okinawa where she landed reinforcements and combat cargo on the 1st May. Later she left, carrying casualties. Thereafter she was busy around the Pacific, carrying troops from San Francisco and Portland, Oregon to Pearl

made them notable. The *Excalibur* was claimed to be the first completely air-conditioned liner (and officers and crew, as well as the passengers, enjoyed this benefit.) The eight verandah suites and all the cabins were outside and all had private facilities. The beds could be easily folded away so that the cabins became quite spacious day-rooms. Public rooms included a dining saloon, a lounge and a smoke room. Décor was in the contemporary American style. Facilities included a swimming pool and a good hospital.

On the 24th September, 1948, the *Excalibur* sailed from New York - or, more precisely, from Jersey City on the other side of the River Hudson - on her maiden voyage. It took her to Marseilles, Naples, Alexandria, Jaffa, Haifa, Beirut, back to Haifa, Alexandria, Piraeus, Naples, Livorno, Genoa, Marseilles, Boston and then home to New York after a round trip of 45 days. But that first voyage highlighted the new difficulties facing companies running to the Eastern Mediterranean. While the ship was at Haifa, the Israeli authorities found that among the cargo she was carrying to Beirut were cases of shotguns and ammunition and barrels of glycerine, all addressed to the Syrian Ministry of Defence. The *Excalibur* was briefly detained and was only released after undertakings were given that the offending items would not be unloaded at Beirut. There was no suggestion, though, that American Export were involved in any illicit activity. The situation became even more difficult when an Arab embargo made it impossible for the ship to trade with both Arab and Israeli ports. The *Excalibur* and her sisters therefore ceased to call at Haifa and Jaffa. For a couple of years, however, the company maintained a separate service to Haifa with the chartered ex-troopship *La Guardia*.

Like many liners running to the Mediterranean, the 'Four Aces' carried a mixture of passengers - port-to-port travellers and leisured Americans taking the round trip as a seven-week cruise. With breathless enthusiasm the company's advertisements hailed the quartet as the 'Newest... Fastest... Finest American-flag passenger liners in the Mediterranean service' - truth to tell there was not much competition for that accolade, but there was some justification for the further gushing claim that 'they provide a new concept of leisurely living at sea in keeping with modern American standards.'

The *Excalibur* very nearly came to a premature end on the 27th June, 1950 when, shortly after leaving her Jersey City pier, she collided in Upper New York Bay with the inward-bound DFDS freighter *Colombia*. The Danish ship burst into

flames and part of her bow was torn away and embedded in the side of the *Excalibur* which began to sink by the head. After her passengers had been removed, the *Excalibur* was beached. Eventually she was refloated and dry-docked for repairs.

In 1951 Istanbul and, on the return leg, Barcelona were added to the itinerary. The following year Istanbul was dropped and calls at Iskenderun and Lattakia were substituted. Later, labour problems began to bedevil American shipping. On one voyage in 1954, the *Excalibur* had to be diverted to Baltimore because of a New York dock strike and in November, 1960 she sailed without passengers owing to a strike of the company's office staff. For several weeks in early 1963, the *Excalibur*, along with much of the rest of the American merchant marine was laid up owing to a Seamen's Strike.

In the late 'fifties the calls at Iskenderun and Lattakia ceased but then a call at Cadiz was introduced on the homeward leg. It was at Cadiz on the 20th October, 1962 that the ship was ordered to leave port owing to a fire in one of her holds. And on the 5th March, 1964 another fire broke out, this time in the galley, and the *Excalibur* was forced to return to New York which she had left the day before. The voyage had to be cancelled.

Passenger ships on the North Atlantic run were among the first to feel the effect of the coming of the jet airliner. This, together with competition to and from some ports from the newer vessels of the Italian and Greek Lines and, to an extent, Zim Israel Lines, led to the withdrawal in 1958 and 1959 of the *Exochorda* and the *Excambion*, leaving the *Excalibur* and the *Exeter* to maintain the remnants of the service.** Then, on 4th November, 1964

---

**American Export Lines had not entirely lost hope for their passenger trade, however. In 1959 they bought American Banner Lines' *Atlantic*. But she was a different kind of ship from the 'Four Aces' - in contrast to their exclusive, all first class passenger lists, the *Atlantic* mainly carried large numbers of tourist class passengers. She also operated on a different route - that to Haifa.

For most of her career with C. Y. Tung's Orient Overseas Line the *Oriental Jade* bore the group's famous plum blossom logo on her funnel. In this view, however, she carries different funnel colours.
*Peter Newall collection.*

the *Excalibur* left New York on her last voyage for American Export. She arrived back on the 16th December.

She lay idle for some time but eventually a buyer was found both for her and for *Exeter* - the great Hong Kong-based shipping magnate, C. Y. Tung. At a time when most other owners were voting with their feet to get out of passenger shipping, he was buying liners at bargain prices. The hope was that, with the consequent low capital costs and with low labour costs too, since he used Chinese crews, he could make them pay. Among the big liners he bought were the mighty *Queen Elizabeth*, American President Lines' *President Cleveland* and *President Wilson*, and American Export's *Atlantic* and, later, *Constitution* and *Independence*. It has to be said that, in most cases, finding profitable employment for these ships proved difficult.

Apparently more successful for a time were his purchases of combination passenger-cargo ships. These included not only the *Excalibur* and *Exeter* but also vessels from the Hamburg America, North German Lloyd and Holland-America Lines and two big 21,000-tonners from

the New Zealand Shipping Co. He ran them in two services, trans-Pacific and Round-the-World, under the name Orient Overseas Line.

Re-named *Oriental Jade* and flying the Liberian flag, the former *Excalibur* left New York on the 21st September, 1965. She arrived at Hong Kong on the 9th November after calls at Los Angeles and San Francisco. Her regular service started in earnest on the 19th November, when she left Hong Kong for Kaohsiung, Keelung, Kobe, Yokohama, San Diego and San Francisco. As was usually the way with combination carriers, she spent several days in some of these ports working cargo and she did not arrive in San Francisco until the 23rd December.

She continued in this service until 1974, registered under the ownership of Atlantic Far East Lines, Inc., one of the many companies in the Tung group. During most of her career with Tung she wore his famous plum blossom logo on her funnel and had Orient Overseas Line painted in large letters along her hull. She suffered occasional mishaps - a fire which destroyed one of her lounges while she lay at her pier in San Francisco in January, 1968 and a couple of minor collisions - but on the whole she served her owner well. Over the years there were occasional variations in her ports of call.

But the days of ships of her kind were numbered. She arrived at Hong Kong for the last time on the 17th January, 1974 and just three days later sailed for Kaohsiung, having been sold to one of the voracious shipbreakers who plied their trade there.

With her bow re-shaped, and with a light grey hull and the familiar Tung funnel colours, the *Oriental Jade* was still a striking-looking ship. *Mark Goldberg collection.*

# 3

# Falstria

**Falstria.**

Completed 1945. 6,993 gross tons. Length overall: 453 ft. 0 ins. Breadth: 63 ft. 2 ins. Draught: 25 ft. 0¼ ins. Single screw. Diesel. Service speed: 15 knots. Became *Veryr*, 1964. Scrapped, 1964.

The *Falstria* was very recognisably a member of an extremely distinguished family of ships. In 1910 A/S Det Østasiatiske Kompagni (i.e.: The East Asiatic Company) of Copenhagen had placed an order with Burmeister & Wain, also of Copenhagen, for the World's first deep-sea motor ship. The performance of the *Selandia*, as she was called, was watched closely by the shipping community and her success sparked off a maritime revolution. East Asiatic themselves went on to introduce a lengthy series of motor vessels, most of them without funnels. Early motor ships very often lacked these appurtenances and discharged the smoke from their diesel engines through slender pipes attached to one of the masts. But, to many eyes, this gave them an emasculated look and before long funnels became the usual thing on motor ships. The East Asiatic Company, however, continued to order funnel-less vessels. The *Falstria* of 1945 was still very much in the distinctive, if quirky, style established by that first *Selandia* years before. Like so many East Asiatic ships she had four raked masts with the twin exhaust pipes affixed to the third.

Like the *Westerdam*, which we shall meet in a later chapter, the *Falstria* took a very long time to complete owing to wartime delays. She was laid down in 1940 and launched in April, 1941 at the Nakskov Skibsvaerft at Nakskov on the Danish island of Lolland. The single 6-cylinder engine came from Burmeister & Wain – where else? Since April, 1940 Denmark had been an occupied country and, on the orders of the Nazis, the *Falstria* was laid up while the shipyard was devoted to more warlike projects. In early 1945 she was attacked by Allied bombers but survived. In May, 1945 the Nazi forces in Denmark surrendered and within six months the ship was completed and ready to enter service.

As their name implied, the main trade of the East Asiatic Company (which dated back to 1897) was 'out

**A typical East Asiatic Co. funnel-less motor ship, the *Falstria* was a very obvious descendant of the famous *Selandia*, the World's first deep sea motor ship.** *Laurence Dunn collection.*

The *Falstria* **started her career on the Baltic – New York route, but was later transferred to the Far Eastern run. She is here seen at Singapore.** *Ambrose Greenway.*

east'. They had also had interests in the North Atlantic trade, however, through the Russian American Line of 1906 onwards and its successor, the Baltic American Line of 1921 – 1930. For some years after that, they retained an interest in the trade as part-owners of the Polish government's new Gdynia-America Line which had bought the Baltic American ships and business. East Asiatic themselves had for many years operated a service to the Pacific coast of North America by way of the Panama Canal and some of these sailings were made via New York. So it was perhaps not too surprising that in 1945, with several new ships coming into service at a time when other owners were desperately short of tonnage and when there was an enormous pent-up demand for cargo and passenger space on the North Atlantic routes, the East Asiatic Company launched a regular service between Northern European ports and New York.

The company's first post-War passenger-carrying transatlantic sailing seems to have been made as early as September, 1945. Two months later, on the 30th November, the brand-new *Falstria* left Copenhagen for New York, where she arrived on the 13th December. It will be obvious from the length of time that she took to cross the Atlantic that the East Asiatic ships were not express liners and, indeed, they were primarily cargo-

carriers – although the best of them also carried a fair number of passengers. In the *Falstria*'s case there was first-class accommodation for 54, later increased to 64. As built, she had 22 double cabins (16 with bathrooms) and 10 singles. Public rooms consisted of a dining room, an impressive domed hall, a children's room, a bar, a lounge and a smoking room which – such were the habits of the day – was several times larger than the lounge. There was also a swimming pool. Cargo was carried in four holds served by both cranes and derricks.

As we have already seen the *Falstria* reached New York on her maiden voyage in December, 1945. She then proceeded to Rosario and Buenos Aires, presumably to load Argentine grain, much-needed in post-War Europe, which she brought back to Danish ports. Thereafter she concentrated on New York sailings. Many of these started at Gdynia before calling at Copenhagen. No doubt the East Asiatic Company saw opportunity in the fact that the Gdynia – America Line was not yet able to re-start its pre-War passenger service. Often, having landed her passengers at New York, the *Falstria* would proceed to Philadelphia, Hampton Roads or Baltimore for cargo. By 1949 the Gdynia calls had virtually ceased. In December of that year the *Falstria* was transferred to the company's main service to the East and her place on the New York run was taken by the slightly bigger *Erria*.

The East Asiatic Company is the Danish equivalent of John Swire and the other historic British trading houses in the East. Like them, it has interests in many other fields than shipping; but, unlike theirs, its sphere of influence has mainly been in Siam, later Thailand, rather than in China. The *Falstria*'s first sailing to the East was typical of the company's main line service. She left Copenhagen on the 21st December, 1949 and spent a month picking up cargo at Gothenburg, Oslo, Hamburg, Middlesbrough, Antwerp and Rotterdam before the voyage began in earnest. There was a call at Genoa and then it was through the Suez Canal and the Red Sea to Colombo, Penang, Port Swettenham, Singapore, Saigon and finally Kohsichang (the roadstead for Bangkok) before heading home. The round voyage, all 22,000 miles of it, took nearly five months. Of course, very few passengers made the entire trip. Most people going east would join the ship at Genoa or, in later years, at Dover or Southampton. The E.A.C. Lines, as East Asiatic was sometimes known in Britain, therefore offered short sea trips to boost passenger revenues. Middlesbrough to Dover (7 days via Antwerp and Rotterdam) cost £32 and upwards in the late 'fifties. Dover to Marseilles or Genoa (7 or 8 days) cost from £33.

In 1951 the *Falstria* made her only voyage on the route to the Pacific West Coast (via New York) and then it was back to the Eastern run. The *Erria* had a bad fire in late 1951 and so in April, 1952 the *Falstria* took her place in the New York service which by now was purely seasonal. Perhaps because of increased competition, she was now taking 10 days on the crossing as against anything between 11 and 13 days a few years previously, which had no doubt been very economical of fuel. She had another spell on the New York run in the Summer of 1953, but otherwise she spent the rest of her career in the eastern service. By now she was usually calling at London on the homeward leg and at the other end of the route she once or twice appeared at Hong Kong and in Japanese and Philippine ports. In 1956, with the Suez Canal temporarily closed, she was diverted via the Cape on three occasions.

For many years the *Falstria* was a very reliable ship but on the 9th July, 1959 she had a serious engine breakdown while making her way along the Red Sea. Another member of the company's fleet, the *Malaya*, was near enough to be sent to her assistance and towed the crippled ship to Suez where repairs took nearly a month. On the 7th February, 1963 the *Falstria* grounded on a breakwater at Ymuiden while heading for Amsterdam. She was refloated the following day, only modestly damaged. But her ill luck was not at an end. While she was being repaired in dry dock at Copenhagen fire broke out in her oil tanks. It could have been extremely serious but fortunately the fire brigade was able to extinguish the blaze after a few hours.

In October, 1964 the *Falstria* arrived back at Copenhagen at the end of her last voyage for the company. She had been sold to Greek-based owners, but not for further service. Now named *Veryr*, she made one final voyage to the Orient – to a shipbreaker's yard at Onimichi

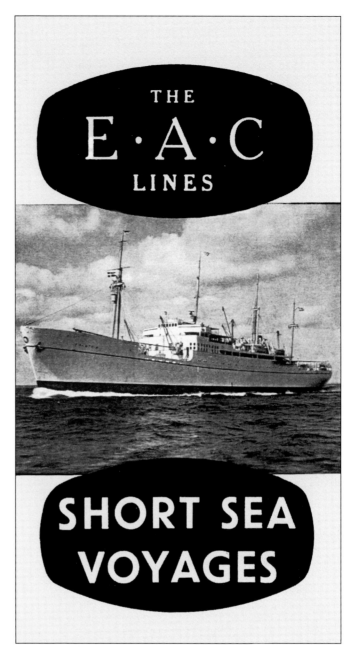

**Before leaving for the Far East, the East Asiatic Co. ships made a round of European ports to load cargo. Passages on this section of the voyage were sold as short cruises.** *Author's collection.*

in Japan. She did not have a long career but there can be no doubt that she, and the other East Asiatic ships, were very fine vessels. Andrew Bell remembers how, as a boy in post-War Australia, he would sometimes see some of the smaller, purely cargo-carrying members of the company's fleet which were then callers at Australian ports. Like the Swedish vessels of the Transatlantic Line, they were regarded as being among the very cream of the ships then to be seen in those parts. Unfortunately, East Asiatic have now more or less given up the shipping business.

# 4

# Laurentia

### Laurentia.

Completed 1945 as *Medina Victory* (7,642 gross tons). Became *Laurentia*, 1947. Converted to passenger ship, 1948-49. 8,349 gross tons. Length overall: 455 ft. 2½ ins. Breadth: 62 ft. 1½ ins. Draught: 34 ft. 6 ins. Single screw. Geared turbines. Service speed: 15 knots. Scrapped, 1967.

In the desperate days after the Second World War, when in Europe almost everything was in short supply - not least ships - a few enterprising owners had standard war-built cargo vessels converted into passenger-carriers in order to participate in the booming emigrant trades. Costa Line's *Andrea C.* had been an 'Ocean' class freighter; several other Italian owners, including Achille Lauro and Emanuele Parodi, used scantily converted 'Liberty' ships to carry migrants for a few voyages; and a number of 'Victory' ships achieved a rather more permanent passenger-carrying status with the Sitmar, Dodero, Jugolinija and Khedivial Mail lines and the Dutch government. The Donaldson Line's two 'Victory' ship conversions were a rather different case from these, however, since they were not an attempt to cash in on the emigrant boom. Instead of providing cheap but crowded

dormitory accommodation for hundreds of travellers, they carried a limited number of passengers in some comfort. (The Alcoa Line of America also used 'Victory' hulls as the basis for combination carriers with high-class passenger quarters.)

The 'Victory' ships were late products of the enormous American emergency shipbuilding programme of the Second World War. Their predecessors, the 'Liberty' ships, of which a mind-boggling 2,710 were completed, were very basic cargo ships welded together from pre-fabricated sections in yards round the coasts of America, many of which had been specially set up for the purpose. The 'Liberties' were intended to be expendable and, running the enemy gauntlet, they made an immense contribution to the Allies' war effort, carrying vital supplies across the oceans. The 'Victory' ships came later and were faster and rather more sophisticated. They were still built in huge numbers by mass-production methods. But, by now scenting that victory might be possible, the Americans planned this new class of freighter partly in order to give useful service after the War had been won.

The *Medina Victory* was one of the later 'Victories' and, like a number of the class, was built from the start as a

**In October, 1947 the former *Medina Victory*, now called *Laurentia*, awaits the fitting of her new, broader funnel while being modified to fit her for Donaldson Line cargo service.** *Laurence Dunn collection.*

**After further rebuilding, the *Laurentia* became a fully-fledged cargo-passenger liner.** *Laurence Dunn collection.*

troop transport. She was assembled at the Permanente Metals Corporation Shipyard No. 1 at Richmond, California, which was one of several yards controlled by Henry J. Kaiser and was one of the most productive shipbuilding facilities the World has ever seen. It had started operations in 1941 and the *Medina Victory*, built in 1945, was already Yard No. 586.

With her stump masts and thin funnel, she was hardly a thing of beauty. The 'Victory' ship design consisted of a five-hold hull of welded construction with two steam turbines driving a single propeller through double-reduction gearing. In *Medina Victory*'s case the turbines were products of the Westinghouse Electric & Manufacturing Co. at Pittsburgh. The ship's one claim to fame was that she was the first American merchant vessel to be built with radar equipment. Fitted out as a troopship, she could carry over 1,500 men. Travelling in a troopship cannot have been a comfortable experience. The 'tweendecks and every other suitable space would be crammed with bunks, perhaps three tiers high. In order to ensure that the *Medina Victory* remained 'blacked out', no portholes were cut into her hull plating lest light should escape and attract the attention of the enemy. On deck, the 'passengers' were crowded together as closely as they were below. The decks carried piles of life-rafts in case the worst happened.

The *Medina Victory* was launched on the 10th February, 1945. Just six weeks later, on the 26th March, she steamed out of San Francisco Bay. Registered at San Francisco and managed for the War Shipping Administration by Marine Transport Lines, she started her maiden voyage from Los Angeles on the 6th April. It took

her to Melbourne, Calcutta, Beira, Durban and Cape Town, and across the Atlantic to New York. Next she was assigned to European duties and, after visiting Southampton and being delayed by boiler problems at Gibraltar, she spent the following months in trooping service round the Mediterranean. In June, 1946 the Americans chartered her to the British Ministry of Transport. Now registered in London, she was placed under the management of Donaldson Bros. & Black Ltd. who ran the old-established Donaldson Line of Glasgow.

Glasgow now became her home port and she visited places as diverse as Mombasa, Naples, Durban and Cuxhaven, repatriating some troops and taking others to fresh duties. Then in April, 1947 she started a series of voyages from Leith to Gdansk. The Communists had just taken over in Poland and the Polish servicemen and other exiles in Britain were bitterly divided. Some decided to return home and it seems probable that the *Medina Victory* carried many of them. Then there followed some voyages from Port Said to German ports, a reminder of just how far-flung the activities of the British army were at that time.

In August, 1947 the Ministry of Transport bought the ship from the American government and a month later they sold her on to the Donaldson Atlantic Line which, as its name implied, ran Donaldson's North American services. She was now registered in Glasgow and re-named *Laurentia*. Barclay, Curle were given the job of stripping out her troop quarters and converting her into a cargo vessel with accommodation for 12 passengers. A new, broader funnel was fitted.

Donaldson Atlantic ran two services - from Glasgow to

Quebec and Montreal; and from Glasgow and Liverpool through the Panama Canal and up the American and Canadian West Coast. It was on this latter route that the *Laurentia* set sail on the 30th December, 1947, arriving back in Glasgow the following April. There followed several voyages on the St. Lawrence route.

Before the War, Donaldsons had run a full-blown passenger service on this route but, like their Anchor Line neighbours with their Glasgow - New York service, they had decided against reviving it. They had sold their one remaining passenger liner, the *Letitia*, to the Ministry of War Transport to become a troopship and, later, emigrant-carrier. However, the Scottish Tourist Board was perturbed at the lack of a direct passenger service from North America to Scotland and it was agreed that the *Laurentia* and the *Lismoria* (another 'Victory' ship which Donaldsons had just purchased) should be given comfortable accommodation for 55 passengers each. Thus the Donaldson Line colours of black funnel with broad white band were once again worn by a pair of transatlantic passenger ships.

Again, the *Laurentia* was sent to Barclay, Curle for conversion. The most obvious external changes were some extension of the superstructure aft, the addition of two extra lifeboats, the felling of the foremast and the substitution of an extra pair of kingposts. The accommodation and facilities provided for the new passengers were of a good standard and were confined to the upper decks. There was a dining saloon, a lounge, two verandahs and a library. Cabins, all first-class, were mainly two-berth but there were a few singles. At a later stage the passenger quarters were air-conditioned.

The *Lismoria* had already started the revived passenger service when the *Laurentia* left Glasgow for Montreal on the 12th May, 1949. Each voyage took eight days and there were occasional calls at Quebec. The ships were still primarily cargo-carriers and therefore spent some days in port between each voyage. Between them, they maintained a more or less twice-monthly service and achieved some popularity. During the winter months, when the St.

Lawrence was frozen, each ship would make a single protracted voyage on the West Coast route - Glasgow - Liverpool - Curacao - Panama Canal - Los Angeles - San Francisco - Victoria - Vancouver and back. Even before the days of the jet aeroplane this was hardly the quickest way of reaching the West Coast, but travellers with time on their hands enjoyed the trip and Peter Telford, who was a Donaldson officer in the latter days*, remembers that these voyages were always fully booked. However, the year-round cargo service on the route was abandoned as uneconomic in 1954 and the *Laurentia* and *Lismoria*'s single voyages ceased after the 1955-56 season. Thereafter, their Winter months were occupied with sailings to Halifax and St. John except for one trip to the West Coast in 1960.

Peter Telford remembers that outward cargo on both routes would include whisky, cars built in the Rootes Group's Scottish factory and chests containing the belongings of people moving from one country to another. Homeward bound from Montreal there would be grain, flour and lumber and, from the West Coast, lumber and some fruit. Bearing in mind the reputation of the Sitmar Lines' converted 'Victories', I asked Peter whether the Donaldson ships were 'rollers'. Apparently not to any worrying extent - perhaps because they had been given less extra superstructure than the Sitmar vessels and, of course, they would be weighed down by cargo. He does remember, though, that they did suffer cracking at the corners of the hatches, particularly on the *Lismoria* - a problem more usually associated with 'Liberty' ships. He also remembers that the passenger quarters had a particularly Scottish look to them, with tartan much in evidence.

The *Laurentia* had her share of minor mishaps, most notably when she was struck by the Cunarder *Saxonia* at Montreal in 1956, but in this and other cases the damage was relatively slight. In 1954, in a reorganisation of the group, ownership of the two ships was transferred from Donaldson Atlantic to Donaldson Line Ltd. In 1966, with trade declining and expensive special surveys looming, Donaldsons decided to quit the passenger business. Both vessels made a few final voyages as purely cargo-carriers and were then sold. The *Laurentia* sailed from Glasgow for the last time on the 28th December, 1966, bound for Valencia for demolition.

---

*and is also the author of a good history of the company and its fleet.

# 5

# Westerdam

**Westerdam.**
Completed 1946. 12,149 gross tons. Length overall: 518 ft. 5 ins. Breadth: 66 ft. 4 ins. Draught: 31 ft. 2³/₄ ins. Twin screw. Diesel. 16 knots. Scrapped, 1965.

In The Times of the 17th August, 1945 there was a brief report - almost everything in the papers was brief in those days since newsprint, like most other things, was in short supply - describing the devastation inflicted on the port of Rotterdam during the Second World War and the efforts which were being made to repair the damage. The situation had been desperate and when Allied ships first brought in food and other urgently-needed supplies the dockers were so weakened by starvation that they were unable to unload them. Before retreating, the Nazi forces had closed the port. 36 big barges had been sunk, side by side, across the river at Nieuwe Merwede and had to be removed before Winter rains caused serious flooding. Other blockships, too, had been sunk along the waterways leading to the port. Lloyd's List noted that one of the sunken vessels, at Merwehaven, was the *Westerdam*. Just ten months later on the 28th June, 1946, that same *Westerdam* left Rotterdam on the first post-War sailing of the Holland-America Line's passenger service to New York. That in itself was remarkable but even more so was the fact that she had been sunk no less than three times.

Her keel had been laid in dry dock at the Wilton-Fijenoord shipyard at Schiedam near Rotterdam in September, 1939. Building ships in docks, although common enough to-day, was then rather unusual. When work started on the *Westerdam*, the Second World War was just beginning. Then in May, 1940 the Nazis invaded and occupied The Netherlands. On the 27th July the *Westerdam* was 'floated out'.

Accounts of what happened to the ship during the War vary bewilderingly. What follows is based in part on an article headed 'From a Rotterdam Correspondent' in the 10th January, 1946 issue of Shipbuilding & Shipping Record. According to this source, the Nazis gave orders that the ship be completed but the Dutch contrived to delay progress and then for a time work ceased altogether because many shipyard craftsmen were taken to Germany for forced labour. Then on the 27th August, 1942 the *Westerdam* was sunk during an air raid by the RAF. It is said that what caused her to settle to the bottom was a large block of masonry thrown out by a nearby explosion which ruptured her hull. She was raised and laid up, heavily camouflaged, but then, in September, 1944, she was sunk again, this time by the Resistance. Once more the Nazis refloated her, planning to scuttle her in the Nieuwe Waterweg, as one of a number of blockships with which they could render the port of Rotterdam inoperable before they were forced to leave. However, in January, 1945 the Resistance struck again, sinking the *Westerdam* themselves where she lay, in a less strategic location. One account says that, after two unsuccessful attempts, they sank her with explosives; another states that they opened her seacocks. Either way, it must have been an act of daring. In Laurence Dunn's collection there is a photograph of the ship shortly before this happened. On the back there is a note that the Resistance sank her just one day before the Nazis planned to do so. It is remarkable that in those desperate times there was someone who not only still had film for his camera but was willing to risk being discovered photographing so important a ship. Finally, in September, 1945, with the Nazis gone and clearance of the port an urgent priority, the *Westerdam* was refloated for the third time and towed to her builders' yard to be cleaned, repaired and completed.

By the 5th June, 1946 she was ready to run her sea

**A clandestine wartime photograph of the uncompleted and much damaged *Westerdam*. She was sunk three times by the RAF and by the Dutch Resistance but was salvaged and completed.** *Laurence Dunn collection.*

**The *Westerdam* and her near-sister, *Noordam*, were purposeful-looking combination liners which maintained Holland-America Line's secondary Rotterdam – New York service.** *Mark Goldberg collection.*

trials, after which she was finally handed over to the owners who had waited nearly seven years for her. It is not quite true to say that the *Westerdam* was the first Holland-America ship to carry passengers across the Atlantic after the War. As early as July, 1945 one of their freighters left Baltimore with about 20 passengers on board. But that first *Westerdam* sailing on the 28th June, 1946 marked the revival of the line's regular passenger service between Rotterdam and New York. On her arrival, under the command of the veteran Captain Thomas Jaski, she was welcomed by the Mayor of the city. Although a combination passenger/cargo ship rather than an express liner in the mould of the glamorous *Nieuw Amsterdam*, there was no doubt that she was well worthy of her place in the service.

When ordered before the War, the *Westerdam* was to have been one of four near-sisters - two for the Rotterdam - New York route; and two, slightly larger, for the service to the Pacific ports of North America. The two New York ships were delivered in 1938 but only one, the *Noordam*, survived the War. (The *Zaandam* was sunk by a U-Boat in 1942, with many lives lost.) The Pacific Coast ships were due to be delivered in 1940 and 1941 but Fate intervened. We have already traced the extraordinary events which the *Westerdam* survived. The fourth ship in the series, the *Zuiderdam*, was also bombed at Rotterdam and, in her case, the Nazis did succeed in sinking her as a blockship. She too was raised but proved to be too far gone to be

restored and completed. So in the end, the two survivors, *Westerdam* and *Noordam*, ran together in a twice-monthly secondary service between Rotterdam and New York, providing a slower but extremely comfortable alternative to the main service,

To ship-lovers the *Westerdam* must have seemed a classic 1940s-style cargo liner, functional but attractive. Less involved observers may have found it more difficult to see beauty in her squat profile, with hardly a raked angle, and her mass of cargo gear. Chacun à son goût. There could be no doubting, though, the high standard of her passenger rooms. Like the equivalent ships of some other companies - Ellerman and the American and German lines, for instance - the Holland-America combination liners carried their limited number of passengers in extremely handsome surroundings. The *Westerdam* could accommodate up to 132 passengers in 54 cabins, including a number of singles and each with its own private facilities. All save one were outside. Concern for passengers' comfort extended to the provision of extra-large beds. The public rooms had been designed before the War by well-known Dutch architects, one of whom had later been shot by the Nazis because of his involvement with the Resistance. A plaque to his memory was placed onboard.

In the words of a Holland-America Line brochure which described the *Westerdam* and the *Noordam* as The One-Class Twins, both vessels had 'exquisitely appointed lounges, as well as a library-writing room, bar, smoking room, enclosed verandah and a large, inviting dining room extending the entire width of the ship. Sweeping sports decks offer ample space for sunning, strolling and outdoor games.' A portable swimming pool could be set up in a cargo hatch on the sports deck. The two ships appealed to a quieter type of passenger who relished the pleasant and uncrowded surroundings, did not require elaborate entertainment and was happy to spend a leisurely 9 days on the transatlantic crossing. Fares on the *Westerdam* were somewhere between those charged for first-class and tourist on the express ships.

In her capacity as a fast freighter, too, the *Westerdam* was well-equipped. With six holds and no less than 24 derricks, including one capable of handling loads of up to 40 tons, she had about 600,000 cubic feet of cargo space, a small amount of which was refrigerated. The ship was driven by two 5-cylinder M.A.N. diesel engines which had been constructed under licence by Wilton-Fijenoord themselves. She was registered at Rotterdam in the name of her owners, Nederlandsch-Amerikaanisch Stoomvaart (Holland Amerika Lijn).

Shipping companies who managed, despite all the difficulties, to be early in the field with passenger sailings in those first post-War years could reap a rich harvest. No doubt the *Westerdam* and the *Noordam* (which came back into service a few weeks after the *Westerdam* made her maiden voyage) were solidly booked. Later, with the *Nieuw Amsterdam* re-starting Holland-America's express service and with the *Veendam* and then the new and mainly tourist class *Ryndam* and *Maasdam* also making regular passenger liner sailings, the *Westerdam* and the *Noordam* established themselves in their own, rather different market.

The pair maintained a very regular service. After arriving at Rotterdam they might occasionally proceed to Antwerp to unload and load cargo; there might be a call at Southampton or a brief stopover in Cowes Roads to pick up passengers; on one or two early voyages, having reached the port of New York, they went upstream to Albany to load grain; there were a few calls at Hampton Roads or at Baltimore. But these were occasional occurrences - mainly the pair were confined to direct sailings between Rotterdam and New York.

In 1963 the *Noordam*, which had had a hectic wartime career as a troopship, was withdrawn and sold. Very briefly the *Westerdam* continued the service in partnership with the *Prinses Margriet*, chartered from the associated Oranje Line. But the era of the combination carrier was almost over. Dock strikes in ports all over the World made it more difficult to maintain regular passenger schedules while at the same time handling cargo. In any case, the commercial jet aeroplane was cutting a swathe through the passenger lists of ships everywhere; and the container revolution was at hand. On the 29th December, 1964 the *Westerdam* arrived in Rotterdam for the last time. She did not linger there very long. On the 29th January, 1965 she sailed for Alicante, having been sold to Spanish shipbreakers.

**The *Westerdam*'s all-first class passengers travelled in considerable comfort, as seen in this view of the Writing Room and Library.** *Charles Zuckerman collection.*

# 6
# Accra

***Accra.***
Completed 1947. 11,599 gross tons. Length overall: 471 ft. 0 ins. Breadth: 66 ft. 2 ins. Draught: 25 ft. 6 ins. Twin screw. Diesel. Service speed: 15½ knots. Scrapped 1967.

Elder Dempster Lines, heirs to two historic concerns which had played an important part in the development of West Africa, were the major British shipping company operating services to that area. As far as passenger traffic was concerned, they had a near-monopoly.

Before the War, their prestige liners were the motorships *Abosso* of 11,000 tons and *Accra* and *Apapa* of 9,000 tons. (Elder Dempster had been among the very earliest exponents of the diesel engine for passenger ships.) All three of these liners were lost during the War and so the company had an urgent claim, in those highly regulated times, to be allotted shipyard berths for the construction of replacements. Initially, two vessels were to be built and the contract went to Vickers-Armstrongs' Barrow yard. Reviving the names *Accra* and *Apapa*, the pair were in later years rather overshadowed by their newer and larger running-mate, the elegant 14,000-ton *Aureol*. But they were good colonial-type liners and, according to Andrew Bell who worked for Elder Dempster in West Africa at one time, they were very profitable to the end of their days.

The *Accra* was launched on the 24th February, 1947 and was handed over to her owners in the September. What Elder Dempster got for their money was, perhaps, a slightly plain-looking ship. It was rumoured that but for the shortage of steel which afflicted Britain in those immediate post-War days, both ships would have been 25 feet longer. There were six holds but much of the hull was taken up by the passenger spaces. Built to cope with long periods of extremely hot and humid weather, both sisters were given two open promenades along each side; there was a permanent swimming pool at the after end of the boat deck, whereas on many ships of this kind the pool was a temporary affair rigged up in one of the hatchways; and all commentators writing about the *Accra* at the time of her introduction were vastly impressed by the large, modern laundry, well able to cope with the needs of her perspiring passengers. Only a few years later, she would have been air-conditioned – and indeed this boon was eventually installed during a 'rolling' programme of work lasting three or four years and completed in 1960. But by the standards of the mid-'forties the *Accra* was, when she was introduced, a very well-equipped hot weather ship.

She could carry up to 245 first class passengers in one- and two-berth cabins, a few of which had an additional Pullman berth, and in a private suite. Very notably for the time, every cabin had either a private bath or shower – whatever she may have lacked in glamour and Atlantic-style bravura, the *Accra* certainly looked after her

**The *Accra* was a plain but purposeful-looking motor ship. At first she had a black hull.** *Ambrose Greenway collection.*

**Later her hull was painted grey, more suitable for her tropical route.** *Ambrose Greenway collection.*

passengers well. She had a dining salon, a lounge, a library, a card room and a smokeroom - the second largest room on the ship, so widespread was smoking in those days. The library contained 'an enclosed cabinet housing an altar piece, so that this room can be used for church services.' There was also a hairdresser's shop. The public rooms were wood panelled and perhaps the most striking decorative feature on board was a frieze in the domed ceiling of the dining salon depicting a West African scene. Later a children's playroom was built into a shaded area on the Promenade deck.

24 third class passengers could be accommodated in 4-berth cabins and when the ship was in West African waters up to 145 coastal travellers could be carried in the fo'c'sle.

Vickers-Armstrongs themselves built, under licence, the two Doxford 4-cylinder diesel engines which drove the ship. The shipping journals in 1947 were particularly intrigued by the air brakes fitted to the shafts which, on trials, proved capable of bringing the ship to a stop in a remarkably short distance. The engines, however, proved troublesome at first and, indeed, on the return leg of the maiden voyage the *Accra* had to put back to Las Palmas for repairs. More serious problems occurred in November, 1949 when she arrived at Liverpool several days late, having completed her voyage on one propeller only, and then spent nearly a month at her builders' yard at Barrow for engine repairs. After that, she had a relatively trouble-free career. She emerged from her stay at Barrow with her hull painted grey instead of the original black, but still with her plain yellow funnel.

The maiden sailing had left Liverpool on the 24th September, 1947 and included calls at Las Palmas, Freetown, Takoradi and Lagos. Occasionally, on later voyages, the ship also called at Accra. The round voyage usually took something under five weeks and the ship would then spend another nine days or so unloading and loading cargo in Canada Dock before returning to the Princes Landing Stage to embark her passengers. She thus left Liverpool every six weeks, usually on a Thursday afternoon. Initially, therefore, the mail ships ran a regular three-weekly service but with the advent of the *Aureol* in 1951 it became fortnightly. In October, 1956, off the Canary Islands, the *Accra* stood by the burning Spanish tanker *Bailen* and eventually took off her crew — most of whom later returned to their ship, however. In 1962 a regular call at the new port of Tema was introduced.

According to Mr. R. I. Walters, Elder Dempster's post-War passenger service was very successful, so much so that when he came to Britain from Nigeria in the late 'fifties the ships were booked so far ahead that he had to travel by the French liner *Brazza* and make his own way from Bordeaux to London. 'Then there was the mail,' he adds. 'Nigeria is a big country and almost all mail came by Elder Dempster. After it had been landed, it used to take three days to clear.'

Times changed, of course, and on the face of it the story of the *Accra* and the *Apapa* is similar to that of so many of the final generation of colonial liners. The Gold Coast achieved independence under the name of Ghana in 1957, followed by Nigeria in 1960, Sierra Leone in 1961

The *Accra*'s card room, like most of her first class quarters, was comfortable rather than luxurious. But she and her sister, *Apapa,* were well-suited to the West African route and were very successful.
*Mark Goldberg collection.*

and the Gambia in 1965. As far as the passenger trade was concerned, there would no longer be the constant flow backwards and forwards of government officials, teachers, missionaries – the people who since Victorian times had served both their own and their adopted countries so devotedly. And to make matters more difficult, these were the years when the airlines, at first with piston-engined aeroplanes and then with jets, were cutting a swathe through the passenger lists of shipping companies everywhere. Also, some of the new and proudly independent countries were forming their own national shipping lines with whom the established companies had to share the available cargo.

But, according to Andrew Bell, the three mail ships in Elder Dempster's extensive fleet continued to be very profitable. 'Cargo was a vital part of the mailboats' earnings – in fact, they could break even carrying no passengers at all. The Mail Service freight rates were not surcharged but they got all the high-paying commodities. Southbound, there were cars (although, frustratingly, there was a limitation on numbers); Guinness in tanks (going to their brewery at Lagos); textiles; specie; machinery; supermarket stocks; and, for bottom weight, bagged salt from ICI. Northbound there was tropical produce (my Morris Minor car reeked of palm kernels after one trip home); all the tin produced at Jos in Nigeria; and ever-increasing amounts of tropical fresh fruit for the U.K.'s Afro-Caribbean market. So valuable was this cargo trade that when the *Accra* was withdrawn the fast cargo ship *Fourah Bay* took her place – and earned even more profit.

'Of course, the passenger trade changed but we were quite successful in filling the spaces left by the old 'colonial' travellers. There were Africans 'doing' Europe and Europeans working for companies in West Africa who could still be persuaded to start their leave with a holiday at sea going north. Then there were the inter-coastal traders, the 'Market Mammies' – formidable ladies who travelled first class, bringing two or three flunkies with them as deck passengers, plus their wares – perhaps, in one direction, bales of sometimes very expensive textiles and, in the other, kola nuts. Such are the complexities of West African trade that other mammies might be taking similar goods in the opposite direction.

'So it was a matter of some disappointment for us when the decision was taken to withdraw the *Accra* in 1967 and the *Apapa* the following year. I think the end was precipitated by the seamen's strike of 1966 and the decision not to go through with the expensive Lloyd's Register/D.T.I. 20-year survey.' Ten years earlier, Elder Dempster had been sufficiently confident of their passenger / cargo service to introduce two extra ships - pre-War 8,000-ton steamers which they bought from Bullard, King who had just closed their passenger service to Natal. They sailed from Tilbury to West Africa for some years.

However, on the 8th September, 1967 the *Accra* left Liverpool on her final round trip, returning on the 9th October. On the 8th November she quit the Mersey for the last time, sailing for a breaker's yard at Cartagena in Spain, where she arrived on the 13th. (The following year the *Apapa* was sold to Far Eastern owners, leaving the *Aureol* to soldier on for a few more years.) Ten years earlier or ten years later the *Accra*, too, would probably have found further employment but the late 'sixties were gloomy times for most passenger lines.

INTERLUDE

# That's why the lady went by tramp

Well, not quite by tramp, perhaps, but certainly not by luxury liner. The story that in 1947 Eva Perón returned to the Argentine from her celebrated 'Rainbow Tour' of Europe on board the 'Victory' ship *Buenos Aires* had always intrigued me. Why did one of the most glamorous and powerful women in the World choose to travel on such a very workaday vessel?

Eva Perón, 'Evita', was the wife of Juan Perón, the Argentine president. She was herself one of history's most famous (or notorious) populist politicians. She was also a beautiful woman with a taste for glamour. During her European tour she had been fêted by presidents and received by the Pope, had fascinated the press with her fabulous gowns and jewels, and had aroused controversy – did she give a fascist salute to a cheering crowd in Rome or did she not? It is said that in a famous Parisian restaurant diners stood on the tables in order to get a glimpse of her. Surely after all that she would have returned in something more exciting than a drab 'Victory' ship? And what did they do to the *Buenos Aires* to make it suitable to carry the country's First Lady (or Leading Lady – she was a former actress)?

Disappointingly, when I investigated the ship's movements they did not tally with the dates of Evita's return. Was the whole thing just another myth? It was only when I learned that Evita and her party had flown from Geneva via Lisbon to Dakar to join the ship and had left it at Recife to fly on to Rio de Janeiro where she was to attend a conference, that things fell into place. But the question remains, why did she travel on such a ship? At the start of her tour she had been flown all the way to Spain in a special DC4 – why not fly all the way back? Or why not travel as a very special passenger on a luxury liner?

It has to be remembered that this was mid-1947. There were no luxury liners on the sea routes from southern Europe to South America at that time. They had all either been lost in the War or had still not returned to civilian service. True, there were a few ships, mainly Spanish or Portuguese, which did have first class accommodation but otherwise such passenger vessels as there were on the route were devoted almost entirely to the carriage of migrants, usually crowded into dormitories. In any case, the President's lady might wish to be seen to be travelling on an Argentine ship. But she made her triumphal return to Buenos Aires on an Argentine vessel anyway, crossing the Rio de la Plata from Montevideo on the famous ferry *Ciudad de Montevideo*.

Two factors may explain the mystery. The plans for Evita's return may have been cobbled together at quite short notice. While she was progressing round the capitals of southern Europe there was still uncertainty as to whether arrangements could be made for her to visit Britain. In the end they couldn't and she didn't. Also, however, it seems that her travel arrangements were in the hands of Alberto Dodero. He was an extremely wealthy man who controlled the Dodero shipping line (Cia.

**The *Buenos Aires* had originally been an American 'Victory' troop transport. The Argentines placed her on the emigrant run from Spain and Italy.** *Steamship Historical Society of America.*

Argentina de Navegación Dodero) and also the company which owned the *Ciudad de Montevideo* – in all, it was said, 382 vessels. Unlike most rich Argentines he was a Perón supporter. He is known to have made a very substantial contribution towards the cost of the 'Rainbow Tour'; and he was a member of the party which accompanied Evita on that tour. What could be more natural than that she should cross the Atlantic by one of his ships?

The Dodero Line had gone into the passenger business soon after the end of the War, cashing in on the massive boom in migration from Spain and Italy to South America. At first they used several 'Victory' ships which the Americans had allotted to the Argentine. The *Buenos Aires* (ex-*Smith Victory*) was one of these. Built as a troop transport, she now carried migrants on her former troop decks. Probably very little was done to improve her troopship accommodation, although the superstructure was extended aft. For a while the Dodero ships ran in conjunction with the *San Giorgio* and the ancient *Santa Cruz* with which the Italian Line was seeking to re-establish its pre-War South American service.

On the 5th August, 1947 the *Buenos Aires* sailed out of Genoa on her second voyage in the new Dodero service. The passengers who crowded her decks were no doubt mainly Italians, either poor or politically compromised, who were seeking a new life in the Argentine which briefly after the War was one of the most prosperous countries in the World. On the 11th August the ship put in at Dakar to pick up some very different passengers – Evita and her party.

According to Guillermo C. Berger of the Instituto de Estudios de la Marina Mercante Iberoamericana, no significant alterations were made to the ship to render it more fit for its famous passenger, apart from the installation of a canvas swimming pool. The captain was required to vacate his cabin for Evita.

Her woman travelling companion was allotted the First Mate's cabin and Alberto Dodero moved into the Chief Engineer's cabin. Other members of the party had also to be accommodated and this presumably precipitated a domino effect as senior officers, displaced from their own cabins, took over the accommodation of their more junior colleagues.

According to one account, Eva Perón did not miss the opportunity of making contact with the emigrant passengers – several hundred future voters. She made a speech to them – or perhaps at them, since she spoke Spanish and they presumably only spoke Italian. However, they were no doubt duly dazzled and fascinated. The ship called at the Brazilian port of Recife on the 15th August. There Eva Perón and her party disembarked and the *Buenos Aires'* brief stint as a 'ship of state' came to an end.

She and her 'Victory' ship running-mates continued to

**Eva Perón crossed the South Atlantic in the converted 'Victory' ship *Buenos Aires* after her famous 'Rainbow Tour' of Europe in 1947.**
*Jim Nurse collection.*

act as emigrant-carriers, after 1949 somewhat overshadowed by the newly-arrived *Corrientes* and *Salta*. (Although conversions of 'Baby Flat-tops', small aircraft carriers based on American C3-type hulls, this pair did at least carry their migrant passengers in cabins rather than dormitories and, outwardly, were smart, modern-looking ships.) In 1952, 24 of the *Buenos Aires'* crew were arrested at Las Palmas and charged with mutiny. Lloyd's noted that the ship was carrying Spanish migrants and indeed in the early 'fifties she did make a number of voyages from Vigo to Buenos Aires, and also some from Hamburg and Amsterdam. In November, 1950 she appeared at Southampton and in September, 1954 she made a trip from Sandefjord in southern Norway to South Georgia (carrying men and supplies to the whaling fleet, one wonders?) Then in 1955 she spent five months in a Genoese shipyard, emerging as a freighter.

The Argentine state bought the Dodero Line in 1949. Then, following the fall of the Perón government in 1955, the *Buenos Aires* and the other Dodero ships passed to the Flota Argentina de Navegación de Ultramar, usually known as Fanu. In 1961 Fanu was merged with another state-owned line to form the Empresa Lineas Maritimas Argentinas. But by now the *Buenos Aires* was no longer needed. She was laid up at Buenos Aires in June, 1962 and the following year she was sold to the Southwind Shipping Corporation of Liberia who re-named her *Fairwind* and used her mainly for trading between the United States and West Africa. In February, 1968 she stranded on Grand Bahama Bank and, judged not to be worth repairing, was sold for scrapping at Bilbao.

As for Eva Perón, on her return to Buenos Aires she was greeted by a vast crowd (a quarter of a million it was said, but who was counting?) while ships sounded their sirens and a plane flew overhead with a welcoming message painted on its wings. She died of cancer in 1952 at the age of thirty-three.

The *Buenos Aires* had been launched as the *Smith Victory* by the Bethlehem Fairfield Shipyard Inc. of Baltimore on the 24th May, 1945. She entered service for the American government's War Shipping Administration that September and was managed on their behalf by Eastern Steamship Lines. She saw only a few months of service as a troop transport before being laid up. In early 1947 she was sold to the Dodero group who registered her in the name of the Compañia Rio de la Plata de Navegación de Ultramar S.A. She had two Westinghouse steam turbines and her dimensions were gross tonnage: 7,604; length overall: 455 ft. 2 ins; breadth: 62 ft. 1³/₄ ins.; draught: 34 ft. 6 ins. As an emigrant ship she could carry 792 passengers. Her service speed was 15 knots.

# Prince George

***Prince George.***
Completed 1948. 5,825 gross tons. Length overall: 350 ft. $^1/_2$ ins. Breadth: 60 ft. 8 ins. Draught: 20 ft. 5$^3/_4$ ins. Twin screw. Uniflow steam engines. 15$^1/_2$ knots. Damaged by fire, 1995 and sank while being towed to the breakers, 1996.

The ships of the state-owned Canadian National Railways may not have been as well-known outside their home waters as those of the rival Canadian Pacific Railway, but they did for many years form an important fleet. In particular, before the War Canadian National owned the 'Lady' boats which ran to the British West Indies. On the west coast they gave their passenger ships 'Prince' names which contrasted with the 'Princesses' of the Canadian Pacific opposition.

By the mid-1940s Canadian National had rather curtailed their shipping activities on the west coast but, nevertheless, in 1946 they placed an order for a new vessel for the cruise service from Vancouver to Alaska. They called the ship *Prince George*, a name which had previously been borne by a famous old three-funnelled coastal liner which had been destroyed by fire the year before. The new *Prince George* was designed by a local Vancouver naval architect, W. D. McLaren, and was built at the Esquimault yard of Yarrows Ltd. She was the largest passenger ship yet built on the Canadian west coast. Perhaps her most notable feature was that she was

The *Prince George,* **wearing her original Canadian National funnel colours, passes under the Lion's Gate Bridge, Vancouver.** *Laurence Dunn collection.*

powered by two 6-cylinder Skinner uniflow engines built by Canadian Vickers at Montreal. (The uniflow was an unusual type of reciprocating steam engine which was claimed to be more efficient because it reduced the amount of steam lost by condensation.) John D. Henderson was Third Engineer on the *Prince George* in 1962. He comments, 'As long as the boiler room gang could keep the steam up there seemed to be no limit to the output the uniflow was capable of.' He also remembers that 'the auxiliary machinery was almost exclusively war surplus. Feed pumps, forced draft fans, fire pumps, sanitary pumps, sludge pumps, steering gear had all been built for wartime 'Town'-class frigates.' John recalls that after the *Prince George* was completed Yarrows put in a claim for additional payment. 'It went to the courts and they were awarded a fair slice of extra cash, as I recall.'

Although primarily a cruise ship, the *Prince George* did have two holds, with a certain amount of refrigerated space. Cars were sometimes carried to Skagway, lifted on and off by crane – as was then normal – and transferred between decks by electric lift.

The bigger 'Prince' ships had always been noted for the high standard of their passenger quarters, and so it was with the *Prince George* which, as might be expected of a Canadian ship, had a great deal of wooden panelling. Intended for sight-seeing, she had a forward-facing observation saloon and open promenades ran along part of the length of her superstructure. She had accommodation for 294 first class passengers. There were two de luxe suites and most of the cabins were twins, but a few were three-berth. The ship could also carry 28 second class passengers, presumably local port-to-port travellers. Because her cargo capacity was limited the *Prince George* had a very short-bowed look. Other features were the ferry-type rubbing strips along her sides and her pointed stern. Her hull was painted black and her funnel had the Canadian National colours of, in ascending order, red, white and blue.

The *Prince George* was launched on the 6th October, 1947, yard number 105. She was completed by mid-1948 and entered service on the 19th June. Hers was a seasonal schedule from April to September or October. Her round trips would take her northwards from Vancouver, heading up the Inside Passage along the coast of British Columbia and Alaska, reaching Skagway before returning. Out of season she might occasionally deputise for the elderly *Prince Rupert* which ran a regular Vancouver – Prince Rupert service, but otherwise she would remain in lay-up throughout the Winter. In the Spring of 1962 she made some voyages from Vancouver to Seattle carrying visitors to the World's Fair.

The *Prince George* acquired a fine reputation over the years. Gilles de Villers sailed on her in 1973. 'By then she was already 25 years old, past her prime but still in good condition. There was so much polished brass and wood on board, a treat for the eye. A fine semi-circular bar overlooked the stern. In the dining room the food was excellent and the service was very good, silverware everywhere.' He also sailed on the rival *Princess Patricia* of Canadian Pacific, and there too standards were very high. He says that, if anything, the food on the *Patricia* was even better than that on the *George*, but the *George* scored by having slightly more comfortable cabins. (In both cases all but 20 or so of the cabins had private facilities and they all had a porthole or a window.) Each ship had its fervent supporters and clearly these were vintage years for cruise passengers along the Pacific coast.

Although she grounded several times and once ran into a cliff, the *Prince George* was on the whole a regular, reliable ship. Her appearance changed little except that in 1963 Canadian National adopted new funnel colours – bright orange-red with the letters CN in large, white, stylised script. For 27 seasons the ship maintained her Alaskan cruise service, but costs were rising. Canadian National announced that the 1975 season would be her last. In fact, the end came sooner than expected. On the 10th April, 1975, a few weeks before her final season was due to begin, she was damaged by fire as she lay at her dock in Vancouver. 20 cabins (or staterooms, to use the North American term) were affected and the season was cancelled. It is ironic that Canadian National's withdrawal from the Alaska cruise trade took place just as it was about to take off. (And, equally ironically, *Princess Patricia* had helped establish a concern which later became one of the most formidable competitors on the Alaskan run – for several winters in the mid-'sixties she was chartered to an American entrepreneur who used her for voyages from Los Angeles to the Mexican coast for a new company which he called Princess Cruises.)

To revert to the *Prince George*, however, all did not seem lost for her in 1975. The provincial government had recently set up a concern called the British Columbia Steamship Company to take over the Canadian Pacific *Princess Marguerite* and her Victoria - Seattle route. They now bought the *Prince George*. At first they bid just $1 Canadian but eventually a deal was struck at $230,000 plus a piece of land. The intention was to use her for a passenger/cargo service up the British Columbia coast. Native Indian artists were invited to submit ideas for the decoration of the ship's exterior with ethnic motifs. The mind boggles! John Henderson recalls that the ship was dressed overall with lights as she lay awaiting conversion. But the whole scheme came to naught - the provincial government fell, the lights were switched off and, eventually, the new administration sold the ship.

The buyers, in 1976, were a firm called Wong Brothers Enterprises, Ltd. who announced their intention of using the *Prince George* as a floating hotel and convention centre at Nanaimo, Vancouver Island. However, things went wrong (or Wong) and the ship lay idly at Nanaimo, apart from a brief period of employment at a pulp mill at Port Angeles. (John Henderson remembers that she was used to provide safe accommodation for management personnel during a particularly acrimonious strike.) Then in April, 1979 she was towed to Portland, Oregon, having been sold to a firm called Luka Holdings, Ltd. for an unspecified use. It remained unspecified and the ship was unemployed until she was repossessed by Wong Brothers in January, 1981 after Luka defaulted on payments due under the purchase agreement.

Again, rescue seemed to be at hand, Although it was now over six years since the *Prince George* had plied the coastal waters, she had not been forgotten. A syndicate of local people formed Canadian Cruise Lines to buy her and bring her back to Vancouver. She was given a $5 million refit and her hull was now painted white with a yellow stripe, edged with blue, at main deck level. The funnel, too, was now white, but with a yellow and blue crown painted onto it. The new owners planned a season of week-long cruises northwards from Vancouver but the first three trips had to be cancelled owing to delays in completing the refurbishment and, more ominously, problems with the boilers. When she did go into service she proved to be so smoky that she was twice charged at Juneau with offences against the pollution laws. Gilles de Villers went on board again during a call at Ketchican in that 1981 season. 'She had been decorated and refurbished in brighter colours. She was spotless but there were problems in the engine room. I believe that by the 1980s not too many competent engineers had experience running her antiquated steam engines and her

Wartime-built Yarrow boilers.' The season was a financial disaster.

Nevertheless, a new company, Canadian Cruise Lines (1982) Ltd., bought her and spent a short half-million dollars on further refurbishment. She now ran back-to-back cruises, one week-long trip going northwards to Skagway, where an air connection was provided, and then another week-long cruise took her back to Vancouver. Once again, the initial round trip had to be cancelled but the rest of the 1982 season was happier and apparently more successful than the previous one. Alas, the following year proved to be a fiasco. Only half the scheduled cruises could be run and in September the Prince suffered the indignity of being arrested for debt.

It would be tedious to list all the hopeful owners through whose hands the *Prince George* passed in the following years. She was moored for a time at Vancouver, then at New Westminster and later in Howe Sound. She did find some employment – a stint as a hotel ship at New Westminster during Expo '86 (with the *Princess Patricia*, also out of work, moored nearby in a similar role); and a charter as an accommodation ship at Valdez in 1989 during the operation to clean up the *Exxon Valdez* oil spill.

**An advertisement for Canadian Cruise Line's unsuccessful attempt in 1981 to revive *Prince George*'s cruise service.** *Gilles de Villers collection.*

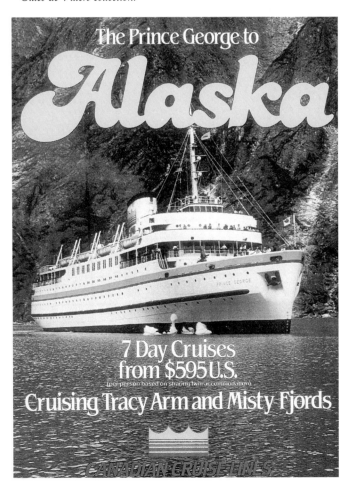

The Mountbatten Observation Saloon, with its wicker furniture, was still in a fairly good state in 1995, even though the ship had been largely unemployed for twelve years. *Peter Knego.*

Many of the public spaces on the *Prince George* were notable for their fine woodwork. *Peter Knego.*

Then, in 1990, there was a brief spell as an accommodation ship for workers on a pipeline being built to Vancouver Island. Thereafter, she lay idly at Britannia Beach, Howe Sound becoming gradually more shabby but earning her owners an occasional dollar or two as a floating 'bed and breakfast'.

Peter Knego visited her in August, 1995 and, indeed, spent two eery nights aboard her. He reported that, although she was badly weathered outside, her interior spaces were in surprisingly good condition. He explored and photographed rooms with names like the Mountbatten Observation Saloon, the Windsor Ballroom, the Prince of Wales Lounge, the Victoria Lounge and the Duke of Kent Room. There were bevelled ceilings,

panelled walls, mirrored pillars, wicker furniture in the observation lounge, a grand staircase with bronze handrails and a dining room 'reminiscent of areas aboard the *Queen Mary*'. It all seems to have been a fine example of the style of the 1940s and '50s. While he was on board, a small fire broke out, due, it seemed, to an electrical short. It was extinguished by the watchman but six weeks later a more serious fire erupted and the ship was virtually gutted. Eventually, in 1996, she was sold for scrapping in China. Some enthusiasts gathered to bid her a last farewell but she was towed away during the night. She never completed that final voyage – she sank during a storm on the 24th October, 1996.

Scarred and forlorn after her fire, the *Prince George* lies at Britannia Beach in October, 1995. *Glenn Smith.*

# 9

# Karanja

### *Karanja / Nancowry*

Completed 1948. 10,294 gross tons. Length overall: 507 ft. 0 ins. Breadth: 66 ft. 3 ins. Draught: 27 ft. 2³/₄ ins. Twin screw. Geared turbine. Service speed: 16 knots. Became *Nancowry* (1976). Scrapped 1988.

The British India service from Bombay to Durban via the East African ports was, more than most, an Empire Route. Sir William Mackinnon, in the second half of the 19th century, was not only the builder of the great British India Steam Navigation Company, but went on to become an Empire-builder – which he no doubt felt to be a patriotic duty. He was one of the men responsible for opening up East Africa and the services which British India developed to and along the East African coast were an important part of his grand design. But while the impetus for the development of the area came from Britain (and Germany), a large individual contribution was made by Indians – labourers, merchants, small businessmen. A considerable passenger and cargo trade therefore developed between the Sub-continent and not only East Africa, but also South Africa. After the Second World War, with India heading for Independence and Partition, the African services, which in the early days had been something of an incubus for the British India company, must have seemed much more promising than the purely eastern routes.

Before the War, the best ships on the Durban Mail, as the Bombay – Durban service was known, had been two steamers built in the early 'thirties and called the *Kenya* and *Karanja*. Both ships were taken up for war service and the *Karanja* was sunk during the North African landings. BI (as British India was often called) did not take *Kenya* back into their fleet after the War and eventually she became the Sitmar Line's *Castel Felice*, one of the stalwarts of the migrant trades to Australia and elsewhere. The replacement of these two ships was a very early priority in the enormous programme of new-building on which BI embarked in order to make good its war losses. As early as 1944 a contract was placed with Alexander Stephen & Son, Ltd. of Linthouse, on the Upper Clyde, for a new Durban Mail ship. Then in 1946, when it became clear that the *Kenya* would not be coming back, a second liner was ordered. Stephen had been the builders of the two pre-War ships and, perhaps because of the urgency of the situation, they now came up with a design which was very noticeably based on the successful one they had produced fifteen years or so earlier.

The first ship, which entered service in 1947, was named *Kampala* and the second was called *Karanja*. They were five-hold vessels, built to carry large quantities of African produce, such as cotton and cashew nuts (an important African export to India), and with a modest amount of refrigerated space. Up to 60 first class

**The *Karanja* in the traditional British India livery at Bombay in 1952. With a passenger capacity of over 1,400, she carried a large number of lifeboats.** *Ambrose Greenway collection.*

The *Karanja*'s first class lounge was a pleasantly furnished room, very much in the 1940s style. *Peter Newall collection.*

Refurbishment in 1969 gave the public rooms a starker style – but passengers now had the benefit of air-conditioning. *Peter Newall collection.*

passengers could be accommodated in single and double cabins on the Bridge Deck. One deck down there was accommodation for most of the 180 second class passengers in 3- or 4-berth cabins. A number of these could, when necessary, be used for additional first class passengers. In the mid-'40s it was not thought in any way remarkable that only two special single cabins had their own facilities and that none were air-conditioned. Typically of British India ships however, the *Kampala* and the *Karanja* carried all first and second class passengers in outside cabins, albeit laid out on the Bibby system in many cases. And both decks had long, shady open promenades – very necessary on such a very hot-weather route.

The two ships were much less luxurious and elegant than the later *Kenya* and *Uganda* which represented British India's final flourish on the more prestigious route from London to East Africa. Undoubtedly, though, they were very comfortable. The first class public rooms consisted of the dining room; a lounge and music room; a verandah café; a smoking room with card room and cocktail bar; and a small library. In addition, there was an airy 'dancing space', which could also be used for showing films. Ted Scull remembers how, when he wished to dance with an Indian girl, he had to ask the permission of her watchful parents. He also wryly comments that when the ship reached Durban, the South African laws decreed that Indian passengers should disembark quite separately from white passengers. Second class public rooms were less extensive but consisted of a dining room, a smoke room with bar, and a music lounge.

The *Kampala* and *Karanja* were very popular with both Indian and British passengers. In part, this may have been due to the fact that they were so much better than the opposition, The Shipping Corporation of India's '*State of Bombay* (unkindly referred to by Ted Scull as the State of Decay' – the sister ship, *State of Madras*, on another route, was the 'State of Madness'). But more than that, the *Kampala* and *Karanja* had all the traditional British India virtues – they were immaculately run, the food was very good 'British Raj', and the much-praised Goanese stewards rendered superb service. (Officers were British,

seamen were Indian and firemen were Pakistani.) In fact, the widely travelled Scull rates the *Kampala* and the *Karanja* as two of his very favourite ships.

With their single tall, steamship funnels and their squared-off superstructures, the pair had a rather stately appearance. Very noticeably, they had no fewer than 28 lifeboats, many of them double-banked. These were necessary because in addition to the first and second class passengers, each ship could carry up to 1,200 unberthed passengers, many of them in spaces which could also be used for cargo. An innovation was that there was also a small 'intermediate' class for those who would normally have travelled in the unberthed section but could afford the slightly greater comfort of a 6-, 7- or 8-berth cabin. Naturally, there were separate galleys for Hindu and Mohammedan food and there was a ritual slaughterhouse. Several former BI officers I have spoken to over the years have claimed that it was part of the company culture that the occupants of this separate, seething lower deck world should be as well cared for as could be managed. Since the *Kampala* and *Karanja* were tropical ships certain precautions were taken and study of the plans reveals that there was an isolation hospital in a separate housing at the stern. And there were padded cells for both males and females unfortunate enough to have 'gone Doolally', to borrow a phrase common among British soldiers in India for generations (i.e.: gone mad).

Stephen themselves built the six Parsons turbines, double reduction geared to twin shafts, which powered each of the two sister ships. Although closely based on the design of their predecessors, the new vessels were more modern in one important way – welding was much more widely used in their construction. The *Karanja* was launched by the wife of a shipyard director on the 10th March, 1948 and ran her trials in September, 1948. She left the Clyde for London (Tilbury) on the 2nd October. There she loaded general cargo for Mombasa, Bombay and Karachi; and took on, it was said, 300 passengers for Mombasa – although how they were all accommodated is not clear. She sailed on the 16th October.

She left Bombay on her first round trip on the 7th

December, 1948 and reached Durban on the 28th, having called at Mombasa, Zanzibar, Dar-es-Salaam, Mocambique, Beira and Lorenzo Marques. On the return leg, she additionally called at the Seychelles and at Mormugão. Over the years, her route varied surprisingly little. Unlike the *Kampala*, which by the mid-'sixties was proceeding only as far as Dar-es-Salaam, the *Karanja* almost always went the whole way to Durban. For some years she called at Karachi on many voyages and left the important Seychelles traffic to the other BI ships, but eventually stops at both were scheduled until the building of a new airport resulted in the Seychelles calls being abandoned. There were, of course, odd deviations from her set route, such as a visit to Cape Town in 1963 to embark Muslim pilgrims whom she carried on part of their journey to Mecca. Also there were voyages to Singapore or Hong Kong for major refits.

*Karanja* proved to be a very reliable ship, suffering few delays due to mechanical problems. There were, of course, incidents such as her arrival at Mombasa in April, 1958 with a case of smallpox on board. She was delayed while 1,800 passengers, crew and dockworkers were vaccinated. In June, 1964, while at Bombay, she developed a sharp list due to covers having been left off several waste pipes. There were two major changes to her appearance. In the mid-'fifties, the hulls of BI passenger ships were re-painted white with a black band instead of the traditional black with a white band. The famous funnel colours were proudly retained, however – black with two broad and closely spaced white bands. Later, changes in Indian government regulations for the carriage of deck passengers resulted in a reduction in the numbers the *Karanja* could accommodate and consequently some of her double-banked lifeboats were removed. Her cabin passengers were now provided with a swimming pool.

The *Karanja* and the *Kampala* were not luxurious and could hardly bear comparison with some of the ships on the routes from Europe to Africa. Nevertheless, for a time their regular voyages were marketed in South Africa as 'cruises' to the Seychelles - outwards on one ship and back on the other. By the 'sixties, though, British India's East African network was beginning to unravel. In addition to the usual factors of independence for former colonies and competition from the airlines, the Durban Mail service suffered the further severe blow of the expulsion of the Asian communities from several East African territories, notably Zanzibar and Idi Amin's Uganda. Nevertheless, the *Karanja* plodded on, although the *Kampala* was withdrawn and scrapped in 1971 and the other ships which had sometimes helped out with the service had also gone. In 1969 the *Karanja* had been given a big refit, claimed to have cost over £1 million. Air-conditioning was installed for her cabin passengers and, in an almost complete refurbishing, the public rooms were furnished in a more modern, rather stark style. She could now carry 493 passengers in various cabin class grades and 408 in a new third cabin class, also air-conditioned and with bunks.

In 1971 the P&O group, of which British India had for decades been a member, was forced to streamline its complicated structure and the few remaining BI passenger ships were transferred to P&O's General Cargo Division, although retaining their BI livery. The Durban Mail run finally petered out on the 9th June, 1976 when the *Karanja* tied up at Bombay after 28 years of very hard service.

Like several other British India ships in those difficult years, including the famous veteran *Rajula*, she was sold to The Shipping Corporation of India. Now called the *Nancowry* and wearing her new owners' funnel colours – black with two yellow bands and spinning wheel badge – she was placed in the service between Madras and the Andaman Islands and was by far the largest ship on the route. She was modified to accommodate 294 saloon class passengers, 200 bunk passengers in air-conditioned quarters and 408 in the old open third class spaces. She persisted in this service until 1988, being scrapped at Bombay in November of that year.

**The *Karanja* in her final form, after her major 1969 refit. She and her sister, *Kampala*, were very popular ships on the India – East Coast of Africa run.** *Ambrose Greenway collection.*

# Marco Polo

*Niccoló Giani | Marco Polo.*
Launched as the *Niccoló Giani*, 1942. Completed as *Marco Polo*, 1948. 8,949 gross tons. Length overall: 485 ft. 0 ins. Breadth: 62 ft. 4 ins. Draught: 25 ft. 11 ins. Single screw. Diesel. Service speed: 15½ knots. Converted into freighter, 1963. 7,026 gross tons. Scrapped 1979.

Like the *Westerdam* and several others, the *Marco Polo* was sunk during the War while still uncompleted but was raised, repaired and finished in the early post-War period. She was a member of a group of six ships which were known as the 'Navigatori' class since they were named after famous explorers. They were among the first new passenger vessels delivered to Italian owners after the War. When planned, however, they had been intended neither to bear navigator names nor to carry large numbers of passengers.

In the late 'thirties, Finmare (the vehicle through which the Italian government controlled the country's four big State-run shipping companies) planned an extensive building programme. Among the projected ships was a group of six freighters for the Italia company, Italia di Navigazione SA (later SpA), which ran the services to North and South America. In English-speaking countries this great company was usually known as the Italian Line.

The six ships, which it was intended should be named after well-known academics, were contracted to be built at the Ansaldo yards at Sestri Ponente, just along the coast from Genoa. The keel of the ship which eventually became the *Marco Polo* was laid on the 12th May, 1940 and she was launched on the 30th May, 1942 as the *Niccoló Giani*** Progress, however, was slow. By 1944 the ship had acquired some superstructure and her two masts but was still far from complete. By now, the occupying German forces were preparing to leave Genoa as the Allies continued their advance up the length of Italy and on the 2nd September, 1944 they scuttled *Niccoló Giani* as a blockship in the harbour. To make her a more difficult obstacle, they ruptured her hull with explosive charges.

The War over, the Italian Line, like shipping companies everywhere, faced up to the problem of how to resume its peacetime services. With most of its passenger liners sunk or temporarily in Allied hands, it decided that the six freighters should be completed as fully-fledged passenger-carriers. The first two entered service as the *Ugolino Vivaldi* and the *Sebastiano Caboto* in 1947. At first their accommodation consisted entirely of large dormitories. Together with the 9,000-ton *San Giorgio* of 1923 and the *Santa Cruz*, a 15,000-tonner which was already 43 years old and had passed through the hands of no less than nine owners, they re-established the Italian

---

**Niccoló Giani was a prominent economist.

**Sunk during the War, the partially-completed freighter *Niccoló Giani* has been raised and awaits completion in 1946-47 as the passenger-cargo liner *Marco Polo*.** *Maurizio Eliseo collection.*

One of the six-member Navigatori class, the *Marco Polo* played an important part in the restoration of Italia's South American services after the War. *Maurizio Eliseo collection.*

Line services to South America. This was a matter of great urgency as a massive migration was taking place from Italy at the time. The third of the six freighters was completed as the passenger ship *Paolo Toscanelli* in 1948. She was given some cabin accommodation as well as dormitories.

Meanwhile, what of the *Niccoló Giani*? In June, 1946 Ansaldo were awarded a contract to raise her and by February, 1947 this had been done. After inspection, it was decided that she was worth repairing and Ansaldo took her in hand and on the 31st July, 1948 they finally delivered her to her owners. She had now lost her original name and was called *Marco Polo*. She could accommodate 698 passengers, 90 of them in cabins and the rest in dormitories. In addition to the usual public rooms she had an outdoor swimming pool and lido. The *Marco Polo* and her sister ships were far from being luxury liners but they served their purpose for some years, taking thousands of Italian and Spanish migrants to new lives in South America.

Cargo was carried in six holds, with some refrigerated space, and there were also deep tanks for vegetable oils. Unusually for an Ansaldo-built ship, the *Marco Polo* was powered not by an engine from FIAT Grandi Motori of Turin but by a 9-cylinder unit built by Stabilimento Tecnico at Trieste. She looked a staightforward kind of ship, with her hull at first painted black and later white.

The 'Navigatori' were intended mainly to revive the service to Venezuela and then through the Panama Canal and on to the ports down the west coast of South America. However, they were also frequently used on the east coast run and several of them were lent at various times to the Lloyd Triestino company to supplement its Australian service. The *Marco Polo*'s first voyage was, in fact, to the

east coast – on the 7th August, 1948 she left Genoa for Naples, Tenerife, Rio de Janeiro, Santos, Montevideo and Buenos Aires. Her second voyage, though, was on her intended route – Genoa, Naples, Barcelona, Cadiz, a nine-day Atlantic crossing to La Guaira, then on to Curaçao and Cristobal and through the Panama Canal to Buenaventura, Guayaquil, Callao, Mollendo, Iquique, Antofagasta, Valparaiso and San Antonio. Between 1948 and 1952 the *Marco Polo* made 17 round voyages on the east coast route and between 1948 and 1963 she made 58 round trips to the west coast. The 'Navigatori' were withdrawn from the passenger service to the east coast in the early 'fifties. They were essentially emigrant ships and by then the Argentine, which had very briefly been one of the most prosperous countries in the World, was no longer so attractive to migrants. Furthermore, the Italian Line were now operating a multi-class express service on the route, using the big pre-War *Conte Biancamano* and *Conte Grande* and, after 1951-2, the new *Giulio Cesare* and *Augustus*.

In 1953 the *Ugolino Vivaldi* and *Sebastiano Caboto* were transferred to the Lloyd Triestino and converted into freighters. The *Paolo Toscanelli* underwent a similar transformation in 1958. This left the *Marco Polo* and the final two members of the sextet, the *Amerigo Vespucci* and the *Antoniotto Usodimare*, to maintain the west coast service. As a young officer with the Pacific Steam Navigation Company, Jim Nurse knew that coast well and remembers calling at a succession of small ports where mooring was made difficult by the heavy Pacific swells and where only modest amounts of cargo were loaded. Passenger/cargo ships like the *Marco Polo* would not visit quite so many ports and, as the voyage records shew, did

The *Marco Polo* spent much of her career on the route from Italy to the west coast of South America. Here she is seen passing through the Panama Canal.
*Enrico Repetto collection.*

*Gugliemo Marconi*, which many people regarded as quite the finest ships on the route between Europe and Australia. They displaced the 12,000-ton *Australia*, *Neptunia* and *Oceania*, which were transferred to the Italia company and took over the service hitherto maintained by the three remaining 'Navigatori'. Now called the *Donizetti*, *Rossini* and *Verdi* ('I Musicisti'), the former Lloyd Triestino vessels were vastly superior – three knots faster, air-conditioned and much more comfortable than the 'Navigatori'.

It was a swap deal – the *Marco Polo* and her two sisters were handed over to Lloyd Triestino and converted into freighters. The *Marco Polo* arrived at Trieste in July, 1963 for work to begin and by January, 1964 she was ready to take up her new career. On 11th January she left Trieste to make a round of Italian ports before setting off for East and South Africa. Her early voyages on the route were via the Suez Canal but after its closure in 1967 she, like so many other ships, had to make the long trek round West Africa and the Cape. In 1967 she made a single voyage to the Far East but otherwise was almost entirely employed on the African route. By the time the Suez Canal was re-opened in 1975 the *Marco Polo*'s career was drawing to a close. She was laid up at Trieste in 1978 and in March that year was sold for scrapping at La Spezia.

not loiter for long when they did call. But essentially, the Italian Line service cannot have been all that different. A round trip, Genoa to Genoa, would take rather more than two months.

The *Marco Polo*'s career was steady rather than eventful, but she was not immune from the strikes which affected the shipping industry in many countries – not least Italy where the state-run lines were particularly vulnerable to political pressures. The worst occurrence was probably in June, 1959 when a national strike of Italian seamen left both her and the *Antoniotto Usodimare* tied up at Cristobal, at the Atlantic end of the Panama Canal, for 40 expensive days.

In later years the *Marco Polo*'s passenger quarters were up-graded. A deck plan dated February, 1960 shews that first class cabins with private facilities could accommodate 86 passengers. And the former dormitories on the lowerdecks had given way to mainly six-berth cabins, no doubt still fairly basic, for up to 432 passengers in so-called tourist class.

It was events elsewhere in the Finmare group which brought about the end of the *Marco Polo*'s career as a passenger liner. In 1963 the Lloyd Triestino company introduced their new 27,000-to *Galileo Galilei* and

**Although primarily an emigrant ship, the *Marco Polo* could also carry a number of cabin class passengers who travelled in some comfort. Here is their dining-room.**
*Paolo Piccione collection.*

# 11
# Caledonia

*Caledonia.*
Completed 1948. 11,252 gross tons. Length overall: 483 ft. 7¼ ins. Breadth: 66 ft. 4¾ ins. Draught: 31 ft. Twin-screw. Diesel. Service speed: 18 knots. Scrapped, 1970.

The Anchor Line of Glasgow, dating back to 1852, was for many decades one of the most important steamship companies on the North Atlantic. In particular, it carried hundreds of thousands of migrants from Scotland, Scandinavia and the Mediterranean to America. Before the First World War it became a subsidiary of the Cunard Line. But the severe restriction of immigration into America in the early 'twenties; and Prohibition, which stopped the import into the U.S.A. of one of the line's major cargoes, Scotch whisky; and then the Great Depression of the 1930s all helped to plunge the company into bankruptcy. The business and the ships were bought by interests connected with Runcimans, one of the major British tramp ship-owning families, in 1935.

In addition to the North Atlantic service, Anchor had for many years been involved in the Indian trade. While the Glasgow – New York service was maintained by modern turbine liners (too many and too large for the remaining trade, in fact), the Indian route was served by some distinctly elderly ships – helped out in the Winter

months by a few voyages by under-employed members of the Atlantic fleet. So, an early priority for the new owners was the building of modern liners for the Indian service. The *Circassia* and the *Cilicia* of 1937 and 1938 were the result and they were fine motor ships of 11,000 tons.

The Anchor Line re-started cargo service on the New York run after the Second World War, but not a full-scale passenger service. Their only surviving Atlantic liner, the *Cameronia*, lay idle for a while and was then used to carry emigrants to Australia and to evacuate Dutch nationals from the East Indies. Further new tonnage was needed for the Indian route, however, and planning began well before the end of the War. It is said that the John Brown yard of Clydebank submitted a design for a 13,000-ton turbine liner but that, in the end, the Anchor Line turned to the Fairfield yard for a third 11,000-ton motorship of the *Circassia / Cilicia* type. The story goes that John Brown thriftily used their Anchor Line design, suitably modified, for the *Patria* and *Imperio* which they completed in 1947 and 1948 for the Colonial company of Lisbon.

The provision of a new ship for Anchor's Indian service was obviously given great priority, since work started in November, 1945 – just two months after the end of the War and at a time when the strict wartime powers which the government had taken to regulate the allocation of

**Wearing the Anchor Line's black livery, the *Caledonia* and her two pre-War sisters were solid motorships which maintained the company's historic Indian service.** *Peter Newall collection.*

**The last passenger ship to be built for the Anchor Line, the *Caledonia* here shews off her cruiser stern and open promenades.** *Ambrose Greenway.*

shipyard berths and to control the supply of steel and other materials were still being exercised. The ship was launched by the Marchioness of Linlithgow on the 12th March, 1947 and was named *Caledonia*, the fifth Anchor Line vessel to carry this suitably Scottish name. She was completed in March, 1948.

The new ship, like her sisters, had a rather foursquare, conservative look, emphasised by the traditional Anchor Line livery of plain black hull and funnel with white superstructure. She looked imposing rather than exciting, but with a pleasingly proportioned profile. As might be expected of a ship which would be plying a hot weather route, she had open, but shady, promenades along the sides of the superstructure. There was an open-air swimming pool and a cinema screen could be slung from the mainmast for outdoor film-shows in the evenings.

There was accommodation for 304 passengers, all in one, first class. Cabins accommodated 1, 2 or 3 passengers and, as was usual at that time, only a very few had private facilities. Similarly, the ship was not air-conditioned – large opening windows, ceiling fans and a punkah louvre ventilation system made life tolerable for the passengers.** The public rooms, furnished in contemporary style and with plenty of wooden panelling, included a striking two deck-high lounge, a dining room, a smoking room, a gallery, a cocktail bar, a verandah café, a hospital and a nursery. Five cargo holds with a total capacity of 442,000 cubic feet were served by 13 derricks. The ship was driven by two four-cylinder Doxford-type opposed piston diesel engines which had been built under

licence by the Fairfield Shipbuilding & Engineering Co., Ltd. Following trials, during which the *Caledonia* sustained 18 knots, it was commented that she was 'practically without vibration throughout the whole of her length at cruising speed' – a noteworthy achievement in a motor vessel. As with most British vessels on Eastern routes, the stewards, engine room staff and deck hands came from the Sub-continent, while officers were British.

The *Caledonia* entered the Indian service in changed times. Independence and Partition would mean that no longer would passenger lists include large contingents of British administrators and Army officers and their families. No longer would 'the fishing fleet' set sail every Autumn – well-connected young ladies being brought out to India by their British families over there in order to find a husband – and no longer would the 'returned empties' – as the ones who failed in the quest were cruelly called – go back to Britain in the Spring. Very occasionally, in an echo of the old days, one of the Indian princes or maharajahs – although now dispossessed of his lands – might book a block of cabins in order to travel with his family and servants. In view of the changed circumstances, the *Caledonia* was given accommodation for slightly fewer passengers than her pre-War sisters, but rather more cargo space. The Anchor liners of the Indian route, although they did not command the prestige of the P.&O. mailships, had a very high reputation as comfortable, immaculately run ships.

---

**Later, however, air-conditioning was installed in the dining room.

Built on the Clyde, like most Anchor Line vessels, and run from Glasgow, the *Caledonia* was a very Scottish ship. Her voyages 'out East' started in Glasgow, where she loaded cargo. She might also visit Cardiff or Avonmouth for cargo, but it was from Liverpool, where she took on yet more cargo and embarked her passengers, that she set out in earnest. On homeward voyages, she sometimes in later years called at the Cypriot port of Limassol, but otherwise she rarely deviated from her direct service between Liverpool, Karachi and Bombay, calling at Aden for bunkers. She usually took about twenty days to reach Bombay. In 1956-7, with the Suez Canal closed, she had to be diverted via the Cape of Good Hope on three occasions. Between the 24th April, 1949, when she left Liverpool for the first time, and the 17th November, 1965 when she made her final arrival there, she achieved a total of 66 round trips.

The most serious accident of her career occurred on the 27th January, 1953 when, during a foggy night in the Suez Canal, she was one of three vessels which collided and ran aground, blocking the waterway. The *Caledonia* suffered relatively slight damage on this occasion and,

indeed, she was not incident-prone. She and her two sisters were solid British ships going about their business in an unsensational way. But it was a shrinking business. Inevitably, with Independence for India and Pakistan came a loosening of the old ties with Britain; and, equally inevitably, more of the cargo trade was carried by locally-owned ships; while by the early '60s the jet aeroplanes were making rapid inroads into the passenger lists.

In 1965 the decision was made to end this historic passenger-cargo service, although the company continued to run break-bulk freighters on the route for a few years more. The final passenger sailing, taken by the *Circassia*, was in January, 1966, but in the meantime the *Cilicia* had been sold for use as a training ship for dockers at Rotterdam; and the *Caledonia* had also been sold for stationary service in the Netherlands – as an accommodation ship for up to 330 students at Amsterdam University. Her appearance was somewhat changed – masts and cargo gear were removed and large, square windows were cut into the hull. She survived until March, 1970 when she was towed to Harburg, slightly up-river from Hamburg, where she was demolished.

**The two-deck high lounge, decorated very much in the style of the mid-1940s and with wood panelling much in evidence, was an imposing room.** *Mark Goldberg collection.*

# Changsha

***Changsha / Kota Panjang.***
Completed 1949. 7,414 gross tons. Length overall: 440 ft.
0 ins. Breadth: 57 ft. 2 ins. Draught: 23 ft. 6³/₄ ins. Single
screw. Diesel. Service speed: 15¹/₂ knots. Became *Kota
Panjang* (1969). Scrapped, 1981.

The China Navigation Company, Ltd. (often referred
to as 'China Nav') has long been a notable British shipping
line. And, unlike many others, it has survived. It has
always been at least partly owned by John Swire & Sons,
Ltd., a private company of London and Hong Kong (and
once of Shanghai). The Swire Group's other interests
include offshore support vessels, a big stake in Cathay
Pacific Airways, Coca Cola bottling, property in Hong
Kong and much else. The origins of China Nav were in the
Yangtze River trade. In the middle of the nineteenth
century Swires began running steamers up the Yangtze, far
into inland China. Over the years, however, they expanded
into coastal and deep-sea shipping. One of their main
services was from the Chinese ports to Malaya, a route on
which they carried large numbers of migrants – the 'coolie
trade' as it was known.

The Second World War, of course, brought all this to
a halt. Afterwards, although now excluded from its former
river and coastal services, the company tried to resume its
pre-War deep-sea operations and embarked on a building
programme to replace the ships it had lost during the
hostilities. However, the Communist takeover of China
ended these hopes. With its operations now centred on
Hong Kong, and with the new ships being delivered, it had
to develop other routes. It had already decided to re-enter
the Australian trade which it had abandoned as long ago as
1912. In that year, the company's Australian agents, G. S.
Yuill, had taken over the service from Chinese ports and
Hong Kong to the Philippines and the ports along the east
coast of Australia. They called their concern the
Australian-Oriental Line. After the Second World War
they resumed the service with their two 4,000-ton
passenger/cargo vessels, the *Taiping* and the *Changte* –
traditional China Nav names, incidentally. But they also
chartered China Navigation Company ships and before
long the service became a joint operation.

Among the ships which China Nav ordered at the end
of the War were three pairs of medium-sized
passenger/cargo liners. In the event, the changed
circumstances meant that it was difficult to find
employment for them all. The two largest, the 9,000-ton
*Chungking* and *Changchow*, never ran in the company's
service, but were chartered for a while to Messageries
Maritimes and then sold to the British Admiralty for

**Despite her uncompromisingly upright funnel, the *Changsha* was a very modern-looking ship. She and her sister *Taiyuan*
gained a good reputation on the Australia – Far East run.** *Peter Newall collection.*

conversion into stores ships. The 6,000-ton *Anking* and *Anshun* were used in various trades, including the Australian run, and with their extensive 'tween-deck accommodation, originally intended for coolies, eventually found employment for part of each year carrying Malayan Mohammedans on the annual pilgrimage to Mecca, disembarking their passengers at Jeddah. It was the remaining pair, the *Changsha* and *Taiyuan*, which had the most settled careers, both being used almost entirely in the Australian service.

They were built by Scotts' Shipbuilding & Engineering Company, Ltd. of Greenock. Some shipbuilders have involved themselves very closely with certain customers, thus ensuring a flow of work for their yards. (Dennys' relationship with the Union Steamship Company of New Zealand, the Henderson Line and the Irrawaddy Flotilla; Harland & Wolff's links with White Star; and Sir William Beardmore's involvement in the affairs of the Lloyd Sabaudo are all cases in point.) From the very early days Scotts had an almost family relationship with Swires and over the years built more than 90 ships for them.

The *Changsha* was launched on the 1st November, 1948, with Lady Masson, the wife of a China Navigation Company director, performing the naming ceremony. By April, 1949 the ship was completed. She was a modern-looking vessel – except for her tall, black, upright funnel. The story goes that the then chairman had very strong views about what a ship should look like, and whenever the designs for a new one were shewn to him he would always insist that the funnel be lengthened. The result was, depending on your taste, either quaintly old-fashioned or a 'proper ship'.

The *Changsha* may have had a steamship-like funnel, but she was, in fact, diesel-powered, by one 5-cylinder Doxford engine built by Scotts. This drove a single propeller. She had five holds, with some refrigerated space to enable her to carry Australian meat. There were 13 derricks, one of which had a 30-ton lift.

Passenger capacity was initially 40 in saloon (in other words, first) class; 42 in tourist (or second); and 70 third. When I described the *Anking* in my previous book, I suggested that she was a rather plainly furnished ship. First class on the *Changsha* had rather more style, at any rate in the public rooms. Heal's had been responsible for these and photographs shew them to have been quite elegant, with the walls and ceilings clad in light-coloured veneers to give an air of coolness. In the dining saloon this was not an illusion since both it and the tourist class dining room were air-conditioned. Elsewhere, the traditional Thermotank punkah louvre ventilation system sufficed. Apart from the dining saloon, first class public rooms consisted of a smoke room; a verandah; and a lounge with a small dance floor, a 'tropicalised' grand piano and a cinema screen which let down from the ceiling. Since a 'swimming tank' was fitted in one of the cargo hatches, the 40 saloon class passengers were obviously rather well provided for. They were accommodated in single- and double-berth cabins, 10 of which had private bathrooms – again, in contrast to the more austere *Anking*.

Tourist class passengers slept in 3- and 4-berth cabins. Their lounge, too, seems to have been pleasantly furnished. The ship had one other facility not so far mentioned – a barber's shop. Kept very separate from the saloon and tourist passengers were the third class, whose mess-room, lounge and dormitories were in the fo'c'sle. As often 'out East', the officers were British and the crew were Chinese.

On the 7th May, 1949 the *Changsha* left the Clyde for Liverpool, where, in Alexandra Dock, she loaded cargo for Australia. She sailed on the 17th May. That first voyage was not the success for which her owners and builders were, no doubt, hoping. She arrived at Gibraltar under tow, having suffered an engine breakdown, and repairs took a week. She finally reached Brisbane (via Adelaide and Melbourne) on the 8th July. Her first voyage in the new Australian-Oriental/China Navigation joint service started from Melbourne on the 23rd July. It took her to Sydney, Brisbane, Manila, Hong Kong, and then on to a round of Japanese ports - Osaka, Kobe, Yokohama and Shimizu - before returning to Hong Kong, Sydney and Melbourne. In all, the round trip took 78 days. On some subsequent voyages there were slight variations, but the route remained basically the same until the mid-'sixties.

Northbound cargoes might include Australian wool for the Japanese market, and meat. On four occasions the *Changsha* called at Geelong to load wheat. As the industries of Hong Kong and Japan got into their stride after the War, southbound cargoes came to include

**Towards the end of her career with The China Navigation Co. the *Changsha* wore their houseflag on her funnel. She is here seen at Melbourne in 1967.** *Ambrose Greenway.*

quantities of manufactured goods. Over the years competition on the route became intense - for instance, from China Nav's lifelong rival The Indo-China Steam Navigation Company, who eventually combined their service with that of another competitor, the Australian-owned Dominion Navigation Company, to form the Dominion Far East Line. Other players included Eastern & Australian Steamship, a member of the P & O group, and the Dutch, in the form of the Royal Interocean Lines.

The *Changsha* had a very eventful career. In September, 1950 she rescued five fishermen from a waterlogged boat off the Chinese coast. Her chief officer was awarded a medal for bravery for his part in the rescue, which took place in a strong monsoon and a heavy sea. Then on the 27th March, 1956 she went aground in Tokyo Bay. Damage was fairly slight but it took 13 days to refloat her and it was not until the 18th April that she was able to resume her voyage. On the 7th October, 1959, again off the Japanese coast, she was swept away by Typhoon Vera and ended up on a sandbank near Nagoya. A channel had to be dug to release her and she was not free until the 11th December. She was dry-docked at Yokohama and repairs were not completed until the 12th

February. On the 18th September, 1960 she suffered a tail-shaft failure after leaving Melbourne and had to return to port.

The withdrawal of the now elderly *Changte* and *Taiping* in 1961 marked the end of the Australian-Oriental Line and henceforth the China Navigation ships maintained the former joint service on their own. For some time they had been calling at Hobart in Tasmania after leaving Melbourne and on their way north they were now in the habit of visiting various other ports on the East Coast besides Sydney and Brisbane. This no doubt helped to fill their cargo holds, but it did lengthen the voyage by several days. In 1964 the ships began to call at Port Moresby on the northward leg, thus strengthening the company's position in the Papua New Guinea trade where it had for some years been challenging the monopoly of Burns, Philp. Further change came in 1965 when the round of Japanese ports was dropped. The route now became outward to Port Moresby and Manila, then on to Hong Kong and directly back to the Australian ports.

Bill Volum travelled on both the *Changsha* and the *Taiyuan* in the 1960s. 'They were spacious, well-run and spotlessly kept, as one would expect with China

Navigation vessels. From a passenger point of view the trip was effectively a cruise. Much of the appeal of these ships was the combination of first class accommodation and service, plenty of deck space (the run of the ship) and not too many people on board, together with an attractive itinerary. Some passengers would book short coastal trips – say, six days from Melbourne to Devonport, Hobart and Sydney. At Hobart the ship first berthed upriver at Risdon to load zinc ingots and then moved downriver to the main wharves at the city centre.' By then, she could accommodate 84 first class passengers and 72 third. Air-conditioning had been extended to some of the cabins.

On the 12th May, 1969 the *Changsha* left Melbourne on her 86th voyage between Australia and the Far East, But she proceeded no further than Hong Kong. The company had decided to withdraw the two passenger/cargo ships from the route, although freighter services would continue. The *Taiyuan* would eventually be transferred to the Australia – Fiji route but the *Changsha* had already been sold. The buyers were Pacific International Lines of Singapore, then very much an up-and-coming company. Mainly known as freighter operators, they did in the late '60s and '70s accumulate a small fleet of passenger/cargo ships. The *Changsha* finally arrived at her new home port of Singapore on the 5th July. She was given the name *Kota Panjang* – most Pacific International ships have had *Kota* names – and was re-painted in the company's house colours of white hull and red funnel with a broad white band bearing the initials PIL in blue.

The *Kota Panjang* was placed in service from Penang and Singapore to Hong Kong and, on some later voyages, Canton – ironically, since years previously the Straits – China run had been one of the mainstays of The China Navigation Company. In 1972 she was joined by her sister, the *Taiyuan* – now also sold to Pacific International Lines, who re-named her *Kota Sahabat*. Competition came from another Singapore company, Guan Guan Shipping, who used small ex-British and ex-Portuguese liners, including the former *Daressa* of the British India Line. The *Kota Panjang* kept going in this service for some years, finally being sold to shipbreakers at

**Now Pacific International Lines' *Kota Panjang*, the former *Changsha* is pictured working cargo at her home port of Singapore in 1973.** *Ambrose Greenway.*

# 13
# Esperia

### *Ausonia / Esperia*

Laid down as the *Ausonia*, 1940. Completed as *Esperia*, 1949. 9,314 gross tons. Length overall: 487 ft. 0 ins. Breadth: 63 ft. 1¼ ins. Draught: 24 ft. 7¼ ins. Twin screw. Diesel. Service Speed: 19 knots. Scrapped, 1975.

She was planned as a successor to a famous Mediterranean liner, the *Ausonia*, whose career had been ended by fire in 1935. That earlier ship, with her deeply curved counter stern and two tall and gracefully raked funnels, had an appearance which hinted at a luxurious 'cruising yacht'. In fact, she participated in a fast and prestigious liner service from Italian ports to Beirut and Alexandria. Beirut was then on of the most elegant cities in the Eastern Mediterranean and many wealthy Egyptians and Italians, on their way to enjoy its pleasures, travelled in the luxurious first class quarters of the *Ausonia*. Towards the end of her brief career she had belonged to the Lloyd Triestino, but by the time her successor was laid down, that company's Mediterranean services had been hived off to a new concern, 'Adriatica' di Navigazione SA.

Adriatica was based in Venice and the symbol of the Lion of Venice was carried boldly on the funnels of its ships. Behind Adriatica, and the other shipping companies owned by the Italian state, lay an organisation called Finmare. In the late 1930s Finmare formulated ambitious plans for the renewal of its fleets. Included in the programme was a new *Ausonia*, for which in 1939 an order was placed with the Cantieri Riuniti dell' Adriatico yards at Monfalcone. According to Maurizio Eliseo, the design was very similar to that of the projected 'Super Victoria', which was intended as a worthy running-mate for the Lloyd Triestino's famous motor liner *Victoria* but which, in the event, was never built. The same team was responsible for the design of both the 'Super Victoria' and the new *Ausonia*.

The keel of the *Ausonia* was laid on the 31st August, 1940 – two months after Italy had entered the Second World War. It seems rather strange that the authorities were willing to allow work to start on a luxury liner at a time when there must have been much more pressing demands upon scarce national resources. Eventually, the

**The completion of the *Esperia* in 1949 was an important step in the re-establishment of the Italian passenger fleet. Despite her rather stiff, upright appearance, she was a notable liner.** *Maurizio Eliseo collection.*

**The first class dining room contained a notable painting by the Italian artist Mario Sironi.** *Paolo Piccione collection.*

decision was taken to complete her as a hospital ship. She was launched on the 20th October, 1941 but fitting her out was obviously not given great priority and she was still in the shipyard when, on 16th October, 1944, she was bombed and sunk during an Allied air raid. These were sad days for the Italian merchant marine – most of their major ships which had so far managed to survive the hazards of war were now either scuttled by the Germans or bombed by the Allies. Almost the only ones which were not sunk were those which had already fallen into American or British hands.★★

Fortunately, once the War was over and the *Ausonia* was raised, it was found that she was repairable. But it was many months before the work of restoration could be completed. Finally, in March, 1949 the ship was ready. At a very late stage she acquired a new name, *Esperia*, (As is well known, the name *Ausonia* was revived some years later for an even finer Adriatica passenger liner, which has more recently had a notable career as a cruise ship run by the Grimaldi family.)

Some Italian ship-lovers feel that the *Esperia* has not received the attention from shipping historians which is her due – perhaps because she was never seen outside the Mediterranean, although it was stated at the time of her completion that she had been planned for both Mediterranean and transatlantic service; she fell just below that magic 10,000 gross ton mark; and, compared with some of the exciting Italian ships of the pre-War years and the elegant liners which Italy produced a few years later, she had a rather stiff appearance. Her tall masts were hardly raked, and neither was her funnel. (That funnel,

incidentally, had a characteristically Italian slope to its top – c.f. the *Saturnia* and the 'Navigatori' class.) But despite her slightly staid look she was a fine vessel and a worthy flagship of a company which acquired an excellent reputation among Mediterranean travellers. She is said to have been a very quiet and smooth-running ship.

Powered by two 10-cylinder Sulzer engines which were products of the shipbuilders' own Trieste facility, the *Esperia* achieved a speed of 22.6 knots on her trials. She had four cargo holds. Interior design was the work of Gustavo Pulitzer Finali who had been responsible for the more avant garde rooms on the great *Conte di Savoia* and who now gave the *Esperia* a very bold modern style. The 150 first class passengers were accommodated in 1- and 2-bedded cabins, some with private facilities. Public rooms for this class consisted of a verandah-belvedere (a much more attractive name for the room than the prosaic English term observation lounge), a dining room, a writing room and two bars. Also, for the first time on an Italian ship (or so it is said) there was a cinema. First class passengers also enjoyed ample open deck space but, surprisingly, there was no swimming pool. Instead, there

★★Of no great relevance to this chapter, but of interest nonetheless, is a hand-written note I came across in an official copy of Lloyd's Confidential Index. It stated that the *Saturnia* and *Vulcania*, outstanding Atlantic liners then in American hands, were to have been allotted to the Greeks as war reparations but that the Americans suggested that, instead, they be handed back to the Italians – a vital factor in the rebuilding of the Italian merchant marine.

were what might be described as play areas of showers and jets.

The *Esperia* also carried up to 80 second class passengers in cabins and 270 third class in cabins and dormitories. In addition, provision was made for 44 deck passengers who, it was thought, might be carried on the run between Alexandria and Port Said. Voyage records shew, however, that as things turned out the ship did not call at Port Said very often.

The introduction of the *Esperia* was a very significant event. She was the first new top-scale passenger liner to be completed for Italian owners after the War. (The 'Navigatori' class ships, one of which, the *Marco Polo*, we have already met, had originally been planned as freighters but were fitted out to carry migrant passengers, mainly in dormitory accommodation. So were the *Sises* and the *Francesco Morosini*.) The new *Esperia* set sail from Trieste on her maiden voyage on the 29th March, 1949. It took her to Venice, Bari and Beirut. On this occasion she went no further, but usually she would proceed to Alexandria. Since Adriatica served both the east and west coasts of Italy there were regular sailings from Trieste by way of Venice, Bari or sometimes Brindisi; and from Genoa and Naples. Very often the ships would alternate, sailing outwards from, say, Trieste and returning to Genoa, or visa versa. Usually, the round trip took 10 days, or 11 if the ship covered the Alexandria – Beirut stretch in both directions.

The advent of the *Enotria* in early 1952 meant that at last the *Esperia* had a worthy, if smaller, running-mate on the route to the Lebanon and Egypt. In 1957 the *Enotria* was replaced by the splendid new *Ausonia* of 11,000 gross tons. It was probably soon afterwards that the *Esperia* had air-conditioning installed for some of her passenger spaces. By now she was sailing mainly out of Genoa and Naples, leaving the *Ausonia* to take most of the Trieste and Venice sailings. Some voyages were now made via Piraeus.

The Egyptian trade may have been affected by the political unrest, and eventually revolution, of the early 1950s and by the Suez crisis of 1956-7, but the *Esperia* continued to sail regularly. For many years her career was remarkably free from incident, but in March, 1962, while she was being docked at Naples, a mooring rope fouled the propeller of the tug *Sesto*, which sank. Then in May, 1964 the *Esperia* grounded outside Alexandria but was soon refloated.

In the 'seventies the Italian state-owned deep sea passenger services were being run down. As a result, Lloyd Triestino's *Victoria* became unemployed. (This was not the famous pre-War *Victoria*, but the one completed in 1953.) She was transferred to Adriatica and took the *Esperia*'s place on the Beirut run. In any case, Adriatica, who had introduced their first ro-ro vessel, the smart passenger / vehicle ferry *Appia*, in 1960, were themselves planning to reduce their conventional passenger fleet. There was no future for the *Esperia* and she was sold to shipbreakers at La Spezia in 1974.

**The *Esperia*'s public rooms, designed by Gustavo Pulitzer Finali, were daringly modern. Here is a first class bar.**
*Paolo Piccione collection.*

# 14
# Leicestershire

### *Leicestershire / Heraklion*

Completed 1949. 8,908 gross tons. Length overall: 498 ft. 0 ins. Breadth: 60 ft. 4 ins. Draught: 27 ft. 6 ins. Single screw. Geared turbines. Service speeds 15½ knots. Became *Heraklion* (1965). Converted to ferry. Sank, 1966.

The family-owned Bibby Line of Liverpool emerged from the Second World War with rather different problems from those faced by most shipowners. At a time when many companies were desperately short of ships with which to resume their pre–War services, Bibby had a surplus of tonnage. The reason was that, among the former colonies of the European powers, Burma was an early starter in the race towards independence and as a result the Bibby Line service from Liverpool to Rangoon was unlikely ever to regain its pre-War levels of activity. In the event, the line found employment for some of its surviving passenger ships by chartering them out for the booming refugee and emigrant trade. Trooping, a traditional Bibby activity, also occupied some of the vessels.

The Burma trade was not abandoned but clearly the days were gone when it could support a fleet of ships able to carry hundreds of passengers. So Bibby's turned to the Fairfield Shipbuilding and Engineering Co., Ltd. of Govan, who had been their chosen builders since the mid-'twenties, for two new vessels which could still handle large amounts of cargo but had accommodation for a rather more modest number of passengers. The new vessels represented a break with the past in another way – throughout the inter-war period Bibby had been devotees of the motor ship, albeit with a steamship profile, but now they reverted to the steam turbine. The two ships were given traditional company names, *Warwickshire* and *Leicestershire*.

Those early post-War years were desperate times for British industry, with shortages of steel and almost every other material and with frequent labour disputes. Fitting out the *Warwickshire* took about twelve months, but things improved and the following year the *Leicestershire* was completed less than six months after being launched. That launch had taken place on the 29th June, 1949. On trials

**The last passenger ship built for the historic Bibby Line service to Ceylon and Burma, the *Leicestershire* is seen here at Aden in 1964. A year later she was withdrawn.** *Ambrose Greenway.*

**The *Leicestershire* spent nearly five years under charter to British India, with whose funnel colours she is seen here.** *Peter Newall collection.*

during December, the ship achieved 18.46 knots over the measured mile, indicating that the required service speed of 15½ knots was well within her reach.

The ship was driven by two turbines, built by Fairfield and double reduction geared to a single shaft. The hull, whose shape had been tested at the National Physical Laboratory, contained five holds which were served by 24 derricks, including one capable of lifting 35 tons.

Whereas pre-War Bibby liners had carried up to 300 passengers, the reduced state of the Burma trade meant that each of the new pair had accommodation for just 80 (and even that proved to be an over-estimate of the likely traffic). They were all-first class ships with one-, two- and three-berth cabins, only two of which had private facilities. All cabins were on the outside; and there was enough space available on the bridge and upper decks to make it unnecessary to employ the system of interlocking L-shaped cabins to which Bibby had given their name in earlier years. The public rooms, panelled and furnished in light colours, consisted of a dining room, a lounge, smoking room, verandah, barber's shop and children's playroom. Ample deck space was

**The former *Leicestershire* under reconstruction into the Greek ferry *Heraklion* in 1965.** *Laurence Dunn.*

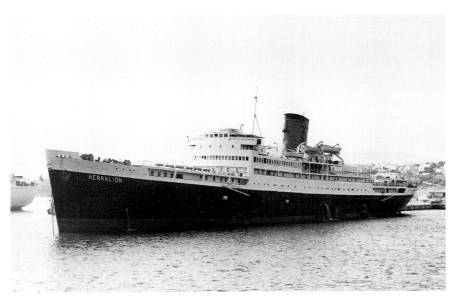

provided and there was a permanent swimming pool, in contrast to the temporary ones let into hatchways which had to suffice on many ships at that time.

Wearing the company's livery of black hull with thin gold band at main deck level and distinctive pink, black-topped funnel, the *Leicestershire* was a well-balanced, modern-looking ship. Two of the pre-War liners, re-fitted to join the new pair in the Rangoon service, not only had their passenger accommodation considerably reduced but were given new profiles, more in keeping with those of their new running-mates – with a short superstructure and a modern, raked funnel. They lost all but one of the four masts which had been a feature of Bibby passenger ships since the 1890s.

The Bibby service is usually thought of as one of two vital links with Burma – the other being the Henderson Line route from Glasgow. But en route, the ships also did a considerable trade with Ceylon, calling at Colombo. Having loaded cargo, including 3,000 tons of cement, at Tilbury and then taken on more cargo at Liverpool, where her passengers were also embarked, the *Leicestershire* started her maiden voyage on the 21st January, 1950. After spending three days at Colombo, she finally arrived at Rangoon on the 20th February.

The return voyage was disastrous – while at Suez on the 26th March, she collided with the tanker *Regent Jaguar*. Much of the *Leicestershire*'s bow was destroyed.

It must already have become clear that the service was over-tonnaged as, after just one more voyage to Rangoon, the *Leicestershire* was chartered to The British India Steam Navigation Company. (Another Bibby ship, the *Herefordshire*, spent ten years under charter to the Port Line.) The *Leicestershire*, now with British India colours on her funnel, left Tilbury on her first voyage in her new service on the 19th August, 1950. She had been placed on BI's main line from London to Port Sudan, Aden, Mombasa, Tanga, Dar-es-Salaam, Zanzibar, Lindi and Beira. On the return leg she would usually disembark her passengers at Plymouth before making a round of British and Continental ports on cargo business. Good ship though she undoubtedly was, she had one disadvantage on this route. Some of the East African ports were terribly congested and very often cargo ships had to wait for long periods before they could get a berth. Passenger vessels were given priority. Unfortunately, the *Leicestershire*, with a

capacity of less than 100, did not qualify. On an extreme occasion early in 1952 she spent 54 days at Mombasa, much of the time lying in the roads, waiting for a berth to become available. Perhaps because of such delays, many voyages terminated at Mombasa.

Nevertheless, she remained with British India for nearly five years being used primarily, one suspects, as a cargo vessel. Handed back to Bibby, she made her return to their Rangoon service in May, 1955. Outward passengers were embarked at Liverpool but homeward they left the ship at London, leaving her free to go wherever cargo was on offer before returning to Liverpool for the start of another voyage. On the outward leg a call would be made at Port Sudan where there were consignments of cotton to be picked up. After the Suez crisis of October, 1956 (during which another Bibby vessel, passing through the canal in a convoy of 17, was one of only four which managed to get out in time) the *Leicestershire* had to be expensively diverted via the Cape on three occasions, adding up to eight days to each voyage. The normal voyage time was between 30 and 33 days. The company withdrew its passenger service in 1965. The *Warwickshire* and the *Leicestershire* had already been sold and on the 27th February the *Leicestershire* left Liverpool for the last time. She now flew the Greek flag and carried the name *Heraklion* on her bow. (As is customary, the name and port of registry on the stern were painted in Greek letters; and the ship was sometimes known as the *Iraklion*, this being an alternative English spelling of the Greek name.) The new owners were Aegean Steam Navigation Typaldos Brothers Ltd. of Piraeus and they intended to convert both sisters into passenger and vehicle ferries. *Warwickshire* was re-named *Chania* (or *Hania*).

Typaldos, perhaps best-known as cruise operators, also ran regular services in the Mediterranean and Adriatic and between Piraeus and Crete. It was for this latter service that the *Heraklion* was intended. Greek owners in those days were noted for their far-reaching conversions of passenger ships and, like some others, Typaldos often carried out the work themselves. In the case of the

*Heraklion* further passenger space was created by filling in the former well deck, extending the promenade deck aft and building cabins and dormitories into much of the cargo space. The ship could now carry 482 passengers in cabins and 192 in dormitories. A vehicle deck was constructed in the forward holds, with access through side doors. The mast and the cargo gear were removed and a signal mast was erected behind the bridge. Despite these alterations, the ship was still quite recognisable as her former self.

By June, 1965 she was in service between Piraeus and the Cretan ports. It was usually a twelve-hour crossing and competition came from the former tankers which Constantinos Efthymiadis had converted into ferries. Unhappily, the *Heraklion* did not survive long in this service. During the early hours of the 8th December, 1966, while making an over-night crossing from Chania in gale-force conditions, she sank. Lorries on the vehicle deck had begun to shift and one of them hurtled into the forward starboard loading door, dislodging it. Within 10 minutes, it was said, of a distress call being sent out the *Heraklion* had capsized and sunk. Greek Royal Air Force planes, American and British naval vessels and many other ships, including the *Chania*, raced to the scene but only 47 survivors could be found. Figures for the number of lives lost varied but it was believed that the total was 241.

A court case followed in February, 1967. Eleven accused had to be protected against an angry crowd trying to get hold of them. Among the defendants were the brothers Spyros and Charalambos Typaldos; a shipbuilder; the first mate and other officers; and officials of the Ministry of the Merchant Marine. Charges included negligence, dereliction of duty and alteration of documents. After a dramatic trial, seven were found guilty, including Charalambos Typaldos. On appeal, however, he and others were acquitted. By then, though, the company was teetering on the brink of ruin and in mid-1968 ceased operations. As a result of the *Heraklion* tragedy, safety regulations for Greek ships were considerably tightened.

# 15

# Baudouinville

***Baudouinville / Thysville / Anselm / Iberia Star / Australasia***
Completed 1950. 10,990 gross tons. Overall length: 505 ft. 0 ins. Breadth: 64 ft. 10 ins. Draught: 27 ft. 6¼ ins. Single screw. Diesel. Service Speeds 15½ knots, becoming 16½ knots after turbocharging, 1957. Became *Thysville* (1956), *Anselm* (1961), *Iberia Star* (1963), *Australasia* (1965). Scrapped 1973.

A great stimulus to the growth of the merchant marine in many European countries was the need to provide links with their overseas empires. In the case of Belgium, lines had to be established to what was then known as the Belgian Congo. The two main companies involved were the Compagnie Belge Maritime du Congo and the Lloyd Royal Belge. In 1930 they merged and the new concern was even-handedly called the Compagnie Maritime Belge (Lloyd Royal), later becoming simply CMB.

Most of the Belgians' colonial passenger ships were of modest size, by far the biggest to sail for the company before the War being the 13,000-ton *Baudouinville* of 1939. She was sunk during the Nazi retreat in 1944, and, although raised, was found to be beyond repair. After the War, the company quickly set about building a completely new passenger fleet, its previous vessels having either been lost or sold to Britain to become troopships. Five liners were ordered from the John Cockerill yard at Hoboken.**

Cockerill-built passenger ships often had a long, low profile, particularly the ferries they produced for the Dover – Ostend service. The five new liners for the Compagnie Maritime Belge also had this look. The name ship of the class, the *Albertville* came out in 1948 and was followed by the *Leopoldville* (also of 1948), the *Elisabethville* (1949), the *Baudouinville* (1950) and finally the *Charlesville* (1951). The last two ships were fitted out to carry slightly more passengers than their earlier sisters – in the case of the *Baudouinville*, 248, all in one class (i.e. first). The passengers were no doubt the usual mix on a colonial route – administrators, businessmen, planters, mining engineers, their wives and children, missionaries. It does seem, though, that, unlike the French and the Portuguese,

---

**Hoboken in Belgium, that is, not in New Jersey – although there were shipyards there too.

**Built for the Belgian colonial service to the Congo, the *Baudouinville* went on to have a very varied career. Here we see her at Tenerife in 1956, still Belgian-owned but recently re-named *Thysville*.** *Ambrose Greenway.*

**Sold to the Booth Line of Liverpool and now called *Anselm*, she saw brief service on the route to North Brazilian ports. This photograph was taken at Lisbon.** *Luís Miguel Correia.*

the Belgians did not make provision for carrying troops in their colonial liners.

Cabins on the two upper passenger decks had private facilities but the much larger number on the lower deck did not. They ranged from a few singles up to four-berth cabins. A number of them had special cots for children. Public rooms included a restaurant, lounge, sitting room, smoke room, bars, a terrace café, a hairdressing salon, a hospital and a chapel. Far aft and rather remote, it would seem, from the rest of the passenger facilities was a swimming pool.

The company had a whole fleet of freighters which it ran to the Congo and elsewhere, but the passenger ships, too, had a large cargo capacity. The *Baudouinville* had six holds served by 16 derricks, including one heavy-lift with a capacity of 40 tons. Some of the 'tween deck space was refrigerated and, since one of the main northbound cargoes was palm oil, there were capacious deep tanks. The ship was powered by an 8-cylinder Burmeister & Wain diesel engine built by Cockerills. This drove a single propeller.

Officers were, of course, Belgian but the crew included some Congolese. The round trip usually took about six weeks. Based at Antwerp, their port of registry, the ships would call at Tenerife before making for Lobito and Matadi. It was at the latter port that most of the cargo was worked. There were also quite frequent calls at Boma, and very occasional ones at Ango Ango and a port with the presumably apt name of Banana.

The *Baudouinville* was launched on the 4th March, 1950. She was completed six months later and in early September made a trial run to Plymouth and back. Her first African voyage started from Antwerp on the 19th September. Over the next eleven years she made a total of 76 round trips.

In 1956 and 1957 the Compagnie Maritime Belge introduced two new 13,000-ton liners into the service. The effect on the *Baudouinville* was two-fold. Her name was required for the second of these new ships, probably because it was thought suitable that the new flagship of the fleet should be called *Baudouinville* in honour of King Baudouin. The existing *Baudouinville*, therefore, had to be re-named and so was called *Thysville*. More importantly, perhaps, the arrival of the new ships, with their slightly higher speed and more modern facilities, precipitated an up-grading of the five original sisters, so as to enable the company to maintain a consistent service.

In May, 1957 the now re-named *Thysville* was taken in hand to have a turbo-charger fitted to her engine, which raised her service speed to 16½ knots, and to have improvements made to her passenger quarters, including the installation of partial air-conditioning. She ran trials, successfully, on the 16th August, and by the 24th August was leaving Antwerp on her first post-refit voyage. Her increased speed shaved two or three days off the duration of each round trip.

On the 13th February, 1958 the *Thysville* had the only serious incident of her Belgian career when she struck bottom quite forcibly near Boma. The jolt caused her to lose some of her deck cargo but damage to the ship herself was not severe and she was able to resume her voyage.

In retrospect, the big investment in improving the

existing ships and in adding new ones to the service seems to have been ill-timed. Political troubles in the Belgian Congo, and then independence, meant that, as on so many of the old colonial routes, traffic dwindled alarmingly.

Early in 1961, after only three and four years of Belgian service, both of the new ships were sold to P & O. Then, the *Thysville* was sold after making her last arrival at Antwerp on the 25th February. The remaining four ships thereafter ran a much-reduced service. In the years following her sale, the *Thysville* had many mechanical problems and one cannot but wonder whether she was singled out as the one to be sold because of suspect reliability.

She remained at Antwerp until the 28th May when, having been bought by the Booth Steamship Co., Ltd., she left for Liverpool flying the British flag and now called the *Anselm*. Booths had for some years been owned by the Vestey family whose shipping interests also included the Blue Star Line and Lamport & Holt. The Booth Line service to Northern Brazil was a very historic one.

The main route was from Liverpool to Manaos, 850 miles up the River Amazon. (Several of the company's small cargo ships penetrated the South American continent even more deeply, however, proceeding as far as Iquitos, a further 1,000 miles upstream.) The main call en route was at Lisbon where, in view of Portugal's historic connection with Brazil, there was cargo to be sought and even, for the passenger ships, a little emigrant traffic. There were also calls at Trinidad and Barbados in order to supplement the modest Brazilian trade. For a time in the 'fifties the line had three passenger vessels, but following the wreck of the *Hilderbrand* in 1957 and the scrapping of the elderly *Hilary* in 1959, only the 1954-built 7,000-tonner *Hubert* remained. The purchase of the *Anselm* reinforced the service, but only briefly.

The grey hull and yellow funnel of her Belgian days gave way to the Booth Line colours of black hull and funnel, the latter bearing the company's houseflag (white with a red saltire and the letter B writ large in blue). The *Anselm* sailed from Liverpool on the 16th June, 1961. The voyage took her to Leixoes, Lisbon, Madeira, Trinidad, Bridgetown in Barbados, Belem and Manaos and lasted two months. Most, subsequent voyages terminated at Belem. Following her purchase her accommodation had been modified to 135 first and 101 tourist. It is said that she proved to be too big for the remaining traffic on the route. Certainly, the casualty report of a fire she suffered at Bridgetown on the 12th January, 1963 mentioned that she was carrying 1,163 tons of general cargo and only 83 passengers. The fire, fortunately, was not serious.

Her stay with the Booth Line was brief. After just 10 voyages ownership was transferred within the Vestey group to Blue Star Line, Ltd., registration was moved from Liverpool to London and the ship was sent to Vegesack, where she arrived on the 28th April, 1963 to be refitted by Bremer Vulkan. Blue Star's service between London and Buenos Aires was being maintained by four 10,000-tonners with considerable refrigerated capacity, intended for cargoes of Argentine meat on the northbound passage, and with good accommodation for 50-odd passengers. Like the famous pre-War 'A'-class liners, these post-War ships carried first class passengers only. The *Anselm* now called *Iberia Star*, was made compatible with her new running-mates. The amount of refrigerated space was expanded and the passenger quarters were re-arranged to accommodate just 76 first class travellers in single and

**Now with more capacity for refrigerated cargo, the recently re-named *Iberia Star* is seen near the entrance to the Royal Docks, London in March, 1964.** *Ambrose Greenway.*

**The much-travelled ship ended her career as the *Australasia* running between Singapore and Australian ports. This photograph was taken as she was leaving Fremantle in May, 1971.** *Nicholas Pusenjak.*

double cabins, all now with private facilities and most with air-conditioning. The swimming pool was now on the top deck, just beyond the funnel. The hull was once again painted grey and the well-known Blue Star colours appeared on the funnel – red with a white disc containing, naturally, a blue star, the whole design surmounted by a black top punctuated by a narrow white band – complicated but distinctive. Because the *Iberia Star*'s funnel was rather short, the white disc, usually almost round, had in her case to be slightly flattened.

She sailed from London on her first Blue Star voyage on the 24th August, 1963. There were calls at Lisbon, Las Palmas, Rio de Janeiro, Santos and Montevideo on the way to Buenos Aires which she reached in 23 days. She had been delayed for 3 days at Lisbon with engine trouble – a portent of future problems. On the 31st July, 1964 she was aground for 15 hours near Montevideo, but without apparent damage. Then there was a further bout of engine trouble in February, 1965. On the 24th September, 1965 the *Iberia Star* returned to London for the last time – once again she had been weighed in the balance sheet and found wanting.

However, the Vestey group had one further option in their search for a profitable use for the ship. They had an offshoot called the Austasia Line which ran between Australia and Singapore. This had started as a cargo operation but early in 1965 the former *Hubert*, now re-named *Malaysia*, was introduced into the service, thus providing passenger sailings. She had been made redundant by the closure of the Booth Line's passenger service. Now, the *Iberia Star*, too, was transferred to Austasia, although ownership remained with Blue Star Line, Ltd. She was now called *Australasia*. For her new

service she once again became a two-class ship, with some of the former tourist class cabins being brought back into use.

Having sailed out to Melbourne via south and East African ports, she set off on her first Austasia Line voyage on the 8th January, 1966. It took her to Sydney, Brisbane, Port Moresby, Singapore and then to Malacca, Penang and Port Swettenham before returning to Singapore and the long haul back to Port Moresby, Sydney and Melbourne. In all, the *Australasia* made 15 of these voyages, sometimes visiting Hobart on the outward trip and also calling at Djakarta. Several times she was delayed by machinery problems.

In February, 1969 she was switched to a new and much shorter route – from the other side of Australia (i.e. Fremantle) to Singapore and sometimes Port Swettenham – leaving the *Malaysia* to maintain the service from the East coast ports. On her new route, the *Australasia* was in competition with the Blue Funnel Line's famous *Centaur*. In 1970 she was transferred to the Singapore flag, no doubt as a cost-cutting measure. She survived on the route for a little longer, but when on the 30th November, 1972 she left Fremantle on her 76th Austasia Line voyage, it was farewell. Her voyage records had become an absolute litany of mechanical problems and, as on so many liner services, the jet aeroplane and the container ship were skimming off much of the traffic. Briefly, the *Malaysia* was switched from the East Coast run to take the *Australasia*'s place, but the end of the passenger service was in sight. As for the *Australasia* herself, within days of arriving at Singapore for the last time on the 7th December, she was towed away to Kaohsiung to be scrapped.

# 16
# Skaubryn

### Skaubryn

Completed 1951. 9,786 gross tons. Length overall: 458 ft. 5 ins. Breadth: 57 ft. 0ins. Draught: 22 ft. 9³/₄ ins. Single screw. Diesel. Service speed: 16 knots. Destroyed by fire and sank, 1958.

The massive migration from Europe in the years following the end of the Second World War drew many shipowners into the passenger business for the first time. Some of them, such as the Costa family, Achille Lauro, Alexandre Vlasov of the Sitmar Line and Evgen Evgenides of Home Lines, were already established in the cargo trades but now saw opportunity for profit in the newly-booming migrant market. One such was I. M. Skaugen of Oslo. He entered the passenger business in 1949 with a vessel which he called the *Skaugum*. She had been laid down as a diesel-electric freighter for the Hamburg America Line shortly before the War broke out and was seized by the Allies, still uncompleted, when it ended. Eventually she passed into Skaugen's hands and, with a pre-arranged charter to the International Refugee Organisation safely in his pocket, he had her converted into a migrant-carrier. Like most of her kind, she was pretty starkly furnished but was regarded as one of the better ships in the trade.

She was sufficiently successful to encourage Skaugen to venture further into the passenger business. Most ships pressed into migrant service in those difficult years were either very old or were conversions – and often they were both. Skaugen, however, was now able to offer a new

vessel which was in effect, purpose-built. True, he had ordered the *Skaubryn* as an open shelter-deck cargo ship from the Oresundsvarvet shipyard at Landskrona in Sweden, but at an early stage he changed his mind – the *Skaubryn* would be an emigrant ship. The hull was launched on the 7th October, 1950 and three days later was towed away by two German tugs to the Howaldtswerke at Kiel. This yard had been responsible for the transformation of the *Skaugum* and had also converted other migrant-carriers. In fact, the tow nearly ended in disaster since the hull broke adrift from the tugs in a very strong wind and, although retrieved, was damaged enough to need dry docking for repairs.

Despite this setback, the ship was completed in February, 1951 and registered jointly in the names of two of Skaugen's companies – A/S Salamis and Dampskip A/S Eikland. She was entirely devoted to passenger-carrying and there were no cargo holds at all. She had a low modern motorship funnel and very little superstructure beyond the bridge. A nine-cylinder diesel engine built by the Gotaverken company of Gothenberg drove the single screw.

Passenger capacity was no less than 1,220, a very large number for a ship of this size. Roughly half of her passengers slept in 4- 6- and 8-berth cabins (without facilities, of course) and the rest occupied separate male and female dormitories. Nevertheless, for many of her early passengers from the refugee camps of northern Germany she must have seemed like Paradise. Almost all this accommodation was within the hull but, in addition,

**Seen in profile, the *Skaubryn*, with her extremely short superstructure, had an unusual appearance. Most of her 1,220 passengers were accommodated within the hull.** *Ambrose Greenway.*

there were just a very few smaller cabins on the bridge deck which could, on occasion, be used for 'first class' travellers.

The *Skaubryn* was, there could be no doubt, a crowded and pretty basic ship but nonetheless she was very well-equipped and was certainly a cut above many vessels in the migrant business. There were three brightly decorated dining rooms which, together with the lounges, were air-conditioned – remarkably for such a ship. Then there were recreation rooms where her passengers could occupy themselves, a swimming pool, a children's playroom (with a miniature ship's bridge, complete with wheel and telegraph) and hairdressing shops. The owner's wife is said to have taken a particular interest in the decoration of the cheerful public rooms, but even there the deckheads were still exposed. The galley was said to be very modern and one frying machine could produce up to 37,000

hamburgers a day (30.328 per passenger!) One hopes that it was never used to the full but, in any case, the *Skaubryn* had particularly good medical facilities.

Mainly white, but with a yellow funnel bearing Skaugen's letter S badge and with a blue riband painted round her bow, she must have looked very smart when she motored into Nordenham, a small port on the Weser, to embark her first passengers. She had been chartered to the International Refugee Organisation (the I.R.O.) for, initially, four voyages. With a virtually full complement of passengers, she left for Australia via the Suez Canal on the 24th February, 1951. She arrived at Fremantle on the 27th March and at Melbourne on the 1st April. Usually, having landed their passengers in their new homeland, I.R.O. ships would return empty. On the Australian run, however, they sometimes returned via the East Indies in order to take on Dutch nationals forced to leave the newly-independent Indonesia. So it was that on the way back to Europe the *Skaubryn* called at Surabaya and then disembarked her unfortunate Dutch passengers at Rotterdam on the 10th May. Subsequent I.R.O. voyages left from either Bremerhaven or Rotterdam and on her third return trip she brought back French troops and other

**In her later years, the *Skaubryn*'s formerly rather stark passenger quarters were very much improved, as seen in these photographs of a typical cabin and one of the dining rooms.** *Mark Goldberg collection.*

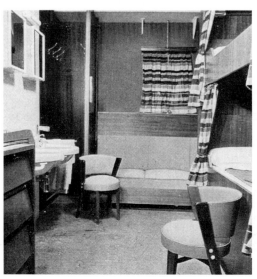

passengers from troubled Indo-China. By 1952, the I.R.O's Mass Resettlement Scheme had more or less been completed and after a few further Australian voyages and one to the Canadian port of Halifax, the ship was returned to her owners.

Further employment had already been found for her, however, under charter to the French government for trooping and other duties between Indo-Chinese ports and Marseilles. Then, in 1953, she was chartered to the famous French company Messageries Maritimes. This historic concern had a very large fleet of passenger and cargo ships, but consistently found it necessary after the War to charter vessels from other owners to supplement its services. Among the passenger ships it employed, often for long periods, were China Navigation's *Chungking* and *Changchow*, The Indo-China Navigation Co.'s *Eastern Queen*, Costa's *Bianca C.* (ex-*Indrapoera*) which became the *Mélanésien* and the former Dutch *Noordam* which was re-named *Océanien*.

The *Skaubryn* was one of the best-equipped of the post-War emigrant ships. Her junior passengers had their own playroom, complete with a miniature ship's bridge.
*Author's collection.*

Now the aristocratic Messageries had joined forces with the nouveau riche Sitmar Line to start a new service from Bremerhaven to Fremantle and Melbourne via Naples or Piraeus. It was claimed to be the first commercial passenger service between northern Europe and Australia since the War. It was a two-ship operation, with the *Skaubryn* running in double harness with Sitmar's *Fairsea*. Emigrant services tended, of course, to be one-way affairs, with ships which had been crowded on the outward leg returning virtually empty. Sitmar's answer to this problem was to try, eventually successfully, to develop a tourist trade. Messageries, on the other hand, were still able to employ the *Skaubryn* on repatriation voyages from Indo-China.

In September, 1955, while on a crowded outward voyage, she suffered propeller damage which at one stage left her crawling along at just 2 to 3 knots. The situation became so serious that water had to be rationed. Attempts to repair the damage at Melbourne while the ship was still afloat caused her to list dangerously and in the end she had to limp all the way back to Brisbane where she was drydocked and fitted with a replacement propeller.

In September, 1956, the *Skaubryn* was chartered by the Dutch government, who were running their own migrant and student-tourist line, for a single Rotterdam – New York voyage via Halifax. Later that year, the temporary closure of the Suez Canal forced her to make the lengthy trek round the Cape of Good Hope on several of her voyages to and from Australia. On some occasions during the mid-'fifties she diverted to Singapore on her return voyages in order to embark British troops whom she brought into Southampton. (While the break-up of the great colonial empires was one of the factors which brought about the demise of the passenger liner, it did at the time provide lucrative employment for a lot of ships.) In the Summer of 1957, the *Skaubryn* was chartered to the Greek Line for four round voyages to Quebec – three from Bremerhaven via Le Havre and Southampton, and one from Liverpool and Greenock. After that, it was back to Messageries Maritimes and the Australia run. By now the public rooms had been improved and, although there was still some dormitory space, most passengers slept in cabins.

Just as today, with so many old, tired and incident-prone ships being recruited for cruise service, one fears some appalling mishap – so in the late 'forties and 'fifties it must have seemed that some of the elderly vessels which were being used in the migrant trades were positively dangerous. It is ironic, therefore, that the most serious incident involving a post-War migrant ship concerned the *Skaubryn*, quite one of the best and most modern of them. On the 15th March, 1958 she left Bremerhaven on another trip to Australia. By the time she had called at Dover and Valletta she was carrying 1,080 passengers (904 under the auspices of the Inter-Governmental Committee for European Migration and 176 passengers privately). On her previous voyage she had been forced to put back to Colombo with engine trouble, but that was as nothing compared to the fate which awaited her on this trip. On the afternoon of the 31st March, heading across the Indian Ocean, she suffered an explosive fire in the engine room. Several ships, including the British frigate *H.M.S. Loch Fada*, the Lauro liner *Roma*, the Ben Line's *Bencruachan*, Ellerman's *City of Sydney*, the *Silverlake* and the Polish *Malgorzata Fornalska* heard her distress call and raced in her direction. Very quickly, much of the *Skaubryn* was engulfed in flames and the order had to be given to abandon ship. This was safely accomplished, although one passenger died of a heart attack. The *City of Sydney* took on board all the passengers and crew, later transferring them to the *Roma* which was better suited to coping with such a large number of unexpected guests. *H.M.S. Loch Fada* took in tow the drifting hulk, whose bridge had collapsed and whose paint had almost completely peeled. Later, she handed over to the tug *Cycloop*. The intention was to take the remains of the *Skaubryn* to Aden, but she was listing increasingly and in the afternoon of the 6th April she sank.

The *Skaugum* had already been withdrawn from passenger service and converted back into a cargo ship. The loss of the *Skaubryn* seemed, therefore, to mark the end of Skaugen's involvement in the passenger trade. Many years later, however, the firm became one of the founding partners in the new Royal Caribbean Cruise Line and, years later still, was for a time part-owner of Pearl Cruises.

# 17

# Índia

### Índia / Kim Hock

Completed 1951. 7,607 gross tons. Length overall: 431 ft. 10 ins. Breadth: 59 ft. 0 ins. Draught: 25 ft. 8 ins. Single screw. Diesel. Service speed: 14½ knots. Became *Kim Hock*, 1971. Scrapped, 1977.

In the period from war's end to the early 'sixties, the Portuguese passenger fleet, once elderly and mainly second-hand, was utterly transformed by an impressive series of new-buildings. Most of these ships were intended for the routes linking the homeland with its overseas possessions, particularly on the west and east coasts of Africa. Further east, the colonies of Goa, Macao and Timor also had their link with Portugal strengthened. In their case, the requirement was for smaller vessels and two 7,000-tonners were accordingly built.

They belonged to the Companhia Nacional de Navegação, the senior of the two biggest Portuguese liner companies – it dated back to 1880, whereas its great rival the Colonial company sprang from the desire of Portuguese farmers in Africa in the 1920s to have their own shipping line. The two ships, called *Índia* and *Timor*, were built by Bartram & Sons, Ltd. of Sunderland on the River Wear in the north-east of England. This aroused comment at the time since Bartrams, although well-known

as builders of cargo ships, had little recent experience of producing passenger vessels. Indeed, the two ships could carry more passengers than any vessels built on the Wear for nearly fifty years. The explanation was that Bartrams were already building two cargo ships for the Nacional company in 1946 when the order for the new vessels was placed. The intention was that they too should be freighters, but at a later stage plans were changed and it was decided that they should be passenger-cargo ships in order to meet the needs of the eastern service.

Progress was slow. Shipyards at that time were inundated with orders and hampered by material shortages and labour disputes. However, the keel of the *Índia*, the first of the pair and yard number 329, was laid on the 1st April, 1949 and the ship was launched on the 17th January, 1950. The hull was then towed to the Tyne where the North Eastern Marine Engineering Co. (1938), Ltd. installed two Doxford 4-cylinder diesel engines. The Nacional company were enthusiasts for Doxford engines, going so far as to specify one some time later for the liner *Niassa* which was built by Cockerill-Ougrée who would normally have installed Burmeister & Wain units. (The Colonial company, on the other hand, tended to favour steam turbines for their passenger ships.) Her engines in place, the *Índia* was towed back to the Wear in late March.

**This view of the *Índia* at Funchal shews off her streamlined superstructure. In the background is the more elderly *Serpa Pinto* of the rival Colonial company.** *Luís Miguel Correia collection.*

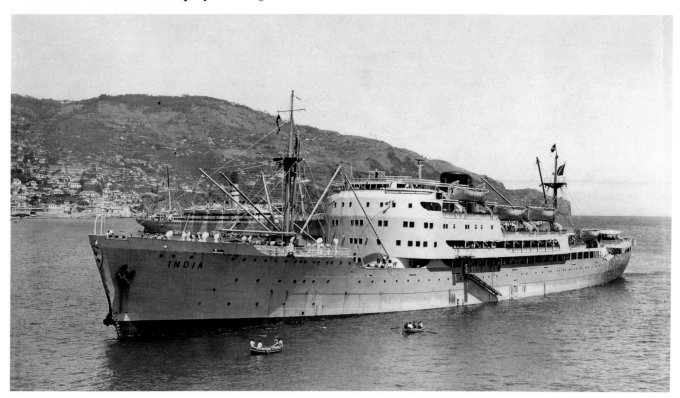

**With her open promenades and her awnings, the *Índia* was very obviously designed for tropical service.** *Ambrose Greenway.*

She was completed in early 1951 and ran her trials on the 3rd and 8th of February. The yard is said to have made a loss on her construction.

Would it be too fanciful to suggest that the Bartram designers relished the opportunity of working on a passenger ship and went out of their way to produce a vessel which, with its raked bow, streamlined superstructure and low, modern funnel, had a certain avant garde style about it? Passenger liner though the *Índia* may have been, she was still a big cargo-carrier and the entire available space in her hull was given over to four large holds which were served by 14 derricks. However, the 'tweendecks in the two forward holds could, when required, be used to carry white emigrants or over 400 unberthed native passengers. Quarters for the first and third classes were confined to the superstructure, with single- and double-berth cabins for 60 first class travellers and 4-berth cabins for 16 third. The twenty best first class cabins, including two forward-facing de luxe suites, had their own private facilities. The usual public rooms were very comfortably furnished in contemporary style with much use of light-coloured wooden panelling. There was very ample deck space, with provision for much of it to be covered by awnings since the ship would be spending a lot of time in the tropics. A large portable swimming pool could be erected over one of the aft hatches. And the ship wore the Nacional livery of grey hull and black funnel.

The *Índia* finally left Sunderland on the 17th February, 1951, calling at Antwerp and Lexões, presumably to pick up cargo, before arriving at her home port of Lisbon. It was not until the 7th April that she started her first outward voyage. There was no very set pattern to the *Índia*'s travels. She made long, wandering voyages to the Portuguese possessions strung out not only in the East but also around the African coasts. Sometimes, garnering cargo, she would make a round of northern European ports before striking off to these more exotic places. That first voyage took her through the Suez Canal to Mormugão, the port for Goa, then back across the Indian Ocean to Lourenzo Marques, round the Cape and up to ports on the west coast, eventually returning to Lisbon after 57 days. The second voyage was a purely west coast affair – Principe, São Thomé, Cabinda, Luanda, Lobito, Mocamedes. The third trip took her out east to Colombo, Singapore and Hong Kong. And so it continued. It was not until voyage no. 6, commencing on the 3rd April, 1952, that she visited Macao. On that trip she was carrying the Portuguese government's Minister for Overseas Affairs.

Evidently Macao was being used as a staging post by European firms trading with Communist China, for in June, 1954 the government of the territory, in accordance with a United Nations embargo, banned the re-export of all 'strategic materials' to China and 'froze' 4,000 tons of cargo which had recently arrived in the capacious holds of the *Índia*. Visits by the two ships to Dilli, the capital port of Portuguese East Timor, amounted to no more than a handful every year but in the early days they did make a number of calls at Philippine ports.

In December, 1954, the *Índia* was involved in a

**The former *Índia,* now the Guan Guan company's *Kim Hock,* was little changed for eastern service.**
*Luís Miguel Correia collection.*

threesome collision at Rotterdam with the Costa Line's *Anna C.* and the *Southern Atlantic,* a freighter. The *Índia* was holed, but not seriously. Increasingly, after 1956 she was used for African voyages, but still with some eastern trips. Following Goa's annexation by India in 1961, visits to Mormugão ceased; and now on voyages Out East the 'tweendecks would be occupied by Portuguese troops on their way to Macao or Timor. According to Luís Miguel Correia, the two ships acquired a bad reputation as a result. Their tank capacity was insufficient for these long, overcrowded voyages and consequently water had be rationed. Furthermore, when the closure of the Suez Canal forced them to cross the vast open spaces of the Indian Ocean, they proved to have stability problems. Nevertheless, the government subsidy which had sustained the eastern service from the outset was being justified. There were also trooping voyages to Bissao in Guinea and to Luanda in Angola.

But Portuguese passenger shipping was petering out and on the last day of 1970 the *Índia* made her final arrival at Lisbon after yet another voyage to Angola. She had been sold to the Singapore Chinese concern Guan Guan Shipping who re-named her *Kim Hock* and registered her in Singapore. Quickly, on the 16th January, 1971, she left Lisbon for her new home port, but via Le Havre, Dakar and Mauritius. On the 20th March, just three days after arriving at Singapore, she set off for Shanghai. More normally, however, she was used on the route from Singapore to Hong Kong and either Foochow or Whampoa. She carried cargo and large numbers of deck passengers, in addition to cabin passengers. Guan Guan were sufficiently pleased with her to purchase her sister ship in 1973 – they called her *Kim Ann.*

The *Kim Hock* remained with Guan Guan for some years, making occasional voyages further afield to such ports as Calcutta, Rangoon and Surabaya, in addition to her regular trips to Hong Kong. Her engines were becoming troublesome, however, and she was sold to Taiwanese breakers in 1977.

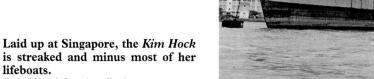

**Laid up at Singapore, the *Kim Hock* is streaked and minus most of her lifeboats.**
*Luís Miguel Correia collection.*

# 18
# Viet-Nam

### *Viet-Nam / Pacifique / Princess Abeto / Malaysia Baru / Malaysia Kita*

Completed 1952. 13,162 gross tons. Length overall: 531 ft. 7 ins. Breadth: 72 ft. 4 ins. Draught: 25 ft. 9³/₄ ins. Twin screw. Geared turbines. Service speed: 21 knots Became *Pacifique* (1967), *Princess Abeto* (1970), *Malaysia Baru* (1971) 11,792 gross tons, *Malaysia Kita* (1972). Damaged by fire, 1974. Scrapped, 1976.

Between July, 1951 and October, 1952 French yards launched no fewer than nine intermediate passenger / cargo liners for Messageries Maritimes. They were basically of similar design but six of them were 17-knot motor ships, either for the route to the French possessions in the South Pacific, and on to Australia; or for the service to Mauritius. The other three, however, were 21-knot turbine steamers for the line to Indo-China, continuing to Hong Kong and Japan.

These faster, Far Eastern ships were no doubt intended to be compatible with *La Marseillaise*, Messageries' 17,000-ton, 20-knot express flagship which had been completed in 1949. However, they were also the company's response to the likelihood of political change in Indo-China which would permanently alter the nature of the old colonial-style service. So they were designed to carry not many more than 100 first class passengers, as against the 341 for whom *La Marseillaise* provided luxurious accommodation. In the event, the three nations of French Indo-China gained their independence in 1954 and in 1957 *La Marseillaise*, having meanwhile been tried on another route, was sold.

The new ships, carrying fewer passengers, had a short-superstructured profile very similar to that of their near-cousins on the other routes. French ship designers like their counterparts in the national motor industry, have not been afraid to give their products unorthodox, often very rounded shapes. In particular, after the advent of the soft bow, French liners sometimes had an exaggeratedly flared front end – *La Marseillaise*, *Antilles* and *Flandre* were cases in point. The designers of the new generation of Messageries liners eschewed these extreme shapes but nevertheless produced nine very modern-looking ships. Each of them had a streamlined funnel with large, grilled apertures fore and aft intended to cause a flow of air which would keep smoke and smuts clear of the after decks. The contemporary Italian liners *Andrea Dora* and *Cristoforo Colombo* had a similar arrangement which was said to be very effective.

The *Viet-Nam* was the first of the Far Eastern trio and was built by Chantiers Navals de La Ciotat, as was the third, the *Laos*. The *Cambodge*, the second ship, was, however, a product of the Dunkirk yard, although the

The *Viet-Nam* and her two sisters, although not as spectacular as some of their predecessors in the Messagaries Maritimes Far Eastern services, were very modern ships. This photograph was taken at Singapore. *Ambrose Greenway.*

The *Viet-Nam* passing through the Suez Canal. The closure of the canal in 1957 and in 1967 caused disruption to a service which was already in decline. *Ambrose Greenway.*

basic design was the work of the Ciotat team. In the early days, La Ciotat yard had actually been owned by Messageries and over a period of more than a century it delivered in excess of 100 ships to them.

The *Viet-Nam* was powered by two sets of three CEM-Parsons geared turbines, built by the Ateliers & Chantiers de Bretagne. She and her sisters were brisk ships but were said at the time to be very economical. According to Louis Cochet, who was a senior Messageries official in the East, '*Viet-Nam*, like *Cambodge* and to a lesser extent *Laos*, were smooth-running ships – except for recurrent troubles, on the first two, with their diesel auxiliaries. The rumour was that they were left-overs from the French Navy's submarine programme – true or not, I can't tell you.' The sisters had a good cargo capacity, with six holds served by eighteen derricks.

Sleek, fitted with stabilisers and extensively air-conditioned, they were in some ways outstanding passenger ships for their time. But, lacking the spectacular oriental-style first class décor of some of the company's liners of previous generations, or the strange square funnels which Messageries affected in the 'twenties and 'thirties, they did not attract as much attention as perhaps they deserved. The interiors of each ship were the work of a different designer and so each sister had a distinct character of her own.

On the *Viet-Nam* there was accommodation for 117 first class passengers in mainly two-berth cabins and in one de luxe suite. All had private facilities and the suite and many of the cabins had balconies – not the first time that these had been widely provided on a liner, but nevertheless an unusual feature. Some of the cabins had attractive lacquered panelling. First class public rooms included a domed dining room, entered in typically French style down a sweeping staircase; a lounge which was also used as the ship's chapel and had a finely decorated altar **; a card room and writing room; a music room and a smokeroom-bar leading out onto a terrace containing the swimming pool. One deck higher was the nursery which opened out at the after end to overlook the swimming pool. According to Louis Cochet, 'In order to avoid any escapes or accidents, the nursery balcony was caged in. My three eldest children, old enough to be slightly naughty,

---

** According to Louis Cochet, 'On the *Cambodge* there were niches on either side of a centre cabinet. Each niche contained a lovely stone statue of a scantily-clad lady. But these statues were not quite what they seemed – they were double faced. On Sundays, when the cabinet became an altar, they were swivelled round and became highly proper statues of St. Joseph and the Virgin Mary. Unfortunately, sacrilegious pranksters delighted in turning them back again and eventually locking systems had to be devised, with the key held by the Second Purser.'

were mad at this and managed to get out. They disappeared into the innards of the ship, including the engine room. We, as parents, learned about it from a furious nurse, scared by the risks they were taking. They also made it a point to visit the kitchens, and particularly the pastrycook – no wonder that at dinner time they were "not hungry".'

110 tourist class passengers could be carried in two- or four-berth cabins without facilities. Their lounge could be converted into a cinema. In addition. there was accommodation for 312 steerage passengers (to quote the old-fashioned term still used by Messageries in some of their English language brochures), mainly in dormitories but with a few cabins. In the early years of the ship's career, much of this space would be used to carry troops.

The *Viet-Nam* was launched on the 14th October, 1951. Construction was slow – French yards, like their British counterparts, were suffering from labour disputes – and it was not until June, 1953 that she was ready to enter service. She had been fitted out at Marseilles. On the 17th July she left that port on her maiden voyage calling at Djibouti, Colombo, Singapore, Saigon, Hong Kong and Yokohama. The round trip there and back, often with calls also at Manila and Kobe, would usually take something over 60 days. At Saigon there would be connections with sailings to ports further north up the Indo-Chinese coast. The Messageries Maritimes liners, on this route painted all-white, were sustained by a postal contract from the French government and by revenues from the carriage of troops. In any case, Messageries (or M.M., as it was known) was a partly-nationalised company.

The closure of the Suez Canal in 1957 and again in 1967 naturally caused the *Viet-Nam* and her sisters to be diverted via the Cape. Also in 1957 they began calling at Bombay and later Karachi and Bangkok were added to the itinerary – no doubt in a search for extra traffic to make up for the decline in the Indo-China trade. This added to the length of the voyage which by 1966 was customarily taking over 70 days. In the early 'sixties all three ships were considerably refitted. The well deck was filled in and third, or steerage, class accommodation was replaced by 'cabin class' consisting of 4- 6- 8- and 10-berth rooms entirely air-conditioned. The air scoops seen protruding from portholes in many photographs of these ships taken out East thus became a thing of the past, except on the crew decks.

The Viet Nam War of the late

'sixties must have caused further disruption of the normal commercial traffic to Indo-China but, in any case, the service was clearly in decline. In 1966, the *Viet-Nam* whose virginal white livery had for some time been adulterated by the addition of the company's flag on the funnel, was used for an experiment which, it was hoped, would fill her empty cabins. It was a time when several shipping companies, desperate to revitalise their liners which had been deserted by traditional long-distance passengers, enlisted the help of holiday firms with 'ideas'. In 1968, for instance, American Export Isbrandtsen, in conjunction with a New York travel agency, converted the *Independence* into a one-class 'fun ship' and painted a psychedelic design on her sides. In the case of the *Viet-Nam*, the holiday trade ally, and the 'idea', were rather more up-market. The ship's first and tourist class space was let to the Club Méditerranée to be turned into a floating version of one of their holiday villages. Sections of the voyage were to be sold as fly-cruises. The project was abandoned after three voyages, the final one of which had to be diverted via Cape Town owing to the Seven Days War and the consequent closure of the Suez Canal.

Thereafter, with the Far Eastern passenger service petering out, the ship was found employment as and where possible. In September, 1967 she left Marseilles on the company's route to the South Pacific and Australia via the Panama Canal, but returned by way of the Cape. She had been re-named *Pacifique*. On her return, she spent four months being refurbished at Dunkirk. In addition to her South Pacific sailings, she also appeared on the run to Mauritius and Réunion, now necessarily via the Cape. But the end was in sight for Messageries' passenger service and the 17th March, 1970 sailing from Marseilles to Papeete,

**First class rooms on each of the three sisters were the work of different designers. Each ship, therefore, had her own style. Here is the salon of the *Viet-Nam*.**
*Mark Goldberg collection.*

Port Vila, Noumea and Sydney was her last for the company. On her return, she was laid up – although reactivated for a handful of short voyages to North Africa under charter to C.G.T. in August.

That month, a buyer appeared. A Hong Kong-based but Panamanian-registered concern, Cia. de Navegación Abeto, took not only the *Pacifique* but also the *Laos*. Abeto had burst onto the passenger shipping scene in quite a major way in the late 'sixties and they collapsed equally spectacularly a few years later. They operated services around the Far East under the name Fir Line but perhaps the mainstays of the business were contracts to carry Indonesian and Malaysian Mohammedan pilgrims to Jeddah, en route for Mecca. They had already bought three former French liners and converted them into pilgrim ships when they purchased the *Pacifique* and the *Laos* and later, in 1972, they acquired another which they ran between Singapore and Fremantle.

The former *Pacifique* lay at Marseilles for a few months before departing on the 11th February, 1971 under the name *Princess Abeto*. It may have been a troubled voyage – it was certainly a slow one, as she did not arrive at Hong Kong until the 18th April. Once safely there, she was converted for her new trade. Her cargo spaces were filled with accommodation for pilgrim passengers and at main deck level the superstructure was extended a long way forward. The deck above this new housing provided an enormous open space – very necessary since the ship now had a passenger capacity of 1,612. Strangely enough, the number of lifeboats seems not to have been increased but, current safety regulations being what they were, one can only assume that other provision was made.

In November, 1971, after a further name change – to *Malaysia Baru* – the ship entered the pilgrim service from Singapore, Port Swettenham and Penang which Abeto now operated in succession to The China Navigation Company. The pilgrim season lasts, at most, only five months and for the rest of the year the Abeto ships would often lie idle at Hong Kong. By the time she started her second season, the *Malaysia Baru* had acquired yet another name – *Malaysia Kita*. Occasionally, while waiting at Jeddah for her passengers to return from Mecca, the ship would make for Massawa or other Red Sea ports to pick up a load of pilgrims from there.

This new career did not last for long. Early in the morning of the 12th May, 1974, while she lay at Singapore undergoing repairs, the *Malaysia Kita* was engulfed by fire. The crew members still on board were rescued and, listing badly, the ship was towed to a special anchorage with the intention that she should eventually be beached. However, she keeled over and continued to burn for five days. Thick, black smoke and leaking oil caused considerable pollution. Salvage attempts on the partly submerged hull started in August but it was not until the following year that it proved possible to raise her. Eventually, she was towed away for scrapping at Kaohsiung in April, 1976. Her sister *Malaysia Raya*, the former *Laos*, was also destroyed by fire, in 1976.

In March, 1975, nearly a year after suffering a devastating fire, the *Malaysia Kita* still lies on her side in Singapore harbour.
*Peter Newall collection.*

# 19

# Baltic Star

**Birger Jarl / Bore Nord / Minisea / Baltic Star**
Completed 1953 as *Birger Jarl*. 3,236 gross tons. Length overall: 304 ft. 0 ins. Breadth: 46 ft. 10 ins. Draught: 16 ft. 1 ins. Single screw. Quadruple-expansion steam engine with exhaust turbine. Service speed: 15 knots. Became *Bore Nord* (1973), *Minisea* (1977), *Baltic Star* (1978). Converted to diesel propulsion, 1982. 12¼ knots. Re-engined again, 1989. Service speed now 14 knots.

As this is written there are two passenger ships called *Baltic Star*. There is a strikingly streamlined German vessel of 2,700 gross tons, built in 1963, which operates day trips from Travemunde; and there is the ship which concerns us here, Panamanian-registered but operating in the Swedish market. Well over 40 years old, tiny by modern standards and with an unashamedly dated appearance, she nevertheless still has a staunch following, despite the fact that the Baltic cruise market has seen the advent (and, in some cases, departure) of some of the biggest and glitziest cruise-ferries ever known.

Not that the *Birger Jarl*, as she was then called, was considered tiny or insignificant when she was built. She was one-third of a three-ship newbuilding programme set in train in the early 'fifties by the companies operating the important routes between Stockholm and Helsinki and between Stockholm and Turku. One reason for embarking on this programme was that it was anticipated that the

1952 Olympic Games, to be held in Helsinki, would create an enormous surge in traffic. In fact, only one of the three ships would be completed in time to participate in this brief boom – the *Aallotar* of the Finland Steamship Company (Finska Ångfartygs). The *Bore III* of the other Finnish partner in the service, the Bore Line, followed later that year; and, finally, the *Birger Jarl* entered service in June, 1953. She belonged to the Swedish company, Stockholms Rederi A/B Svea.

The three ships, which came from different builders, were similar but were not exact sisters. In each case, however, the engine, a product of the Danish company Helsingor Skibsvaerft, was a single 4-cylinder quadruple-expansion steam unit augmented by an exhaust turbine. The *Birger Jarl* was built at Stockholm by A/B Finnboda Varf, which was a member of the same group as the ship's owners. She was yard number 351. Naturally, her hull was strengthened for navigation in ice. Primarily a passenger ship, the *Birger Jarl* did have one hold for cargo. As built, she could accommodate 57 first and 219 second class passengers in small cabins, plus a further 600 day passengers. There was comment at the time on the high standard of the interior furnishing and on the work of Swedish artists displayed on board. Safety precautions also received favourable mention, notably the sprinkler system which in cold weather could be maintained with warm water to prevent freezing.

**Five stages in the career of the *Baltic Star*: 1. As the Svea Line's ferry *Birger Jarl*.** *Ambrose Greenway.*

In the 1950s the services between Stockholm and the Finnish ports were jointly run by two Finnish companies and one Swedish. *Peter Newall collection.*

The *Birger Jarl* was launched on the 15th January, 1953 and entered service on the 9th June, initially on the Stockholm - Helsinki run. Over the years, she was also used on the Stockholm to Turku route via Mariehamn. Passenger shipping formed only a part of the Svea company's activities – in 1953 it and its associated concerns owned about 53 vessels, mainly small freighters. Nevertheless, the ferry services between Sweden and Finland must have been one of the fastest growing elements in the group. Traffic increased at a brisk rate and by the early 'sixties the three partners were introducing bigger ships which could offer drive on/drive off facilities for the growing number of passengers who wished to take their cars with them. Soon, even bigger ferries were needed, capable of carrying a vastly larger number of cars, and also lorries and coaches. The Svea, Finska and Bore companies already had a joint subsidiary called the Siljarederiet (or Silja Line, which means Seal Line) and in 1970 all operations on the Helsinki and Turku routes were concentrated in this company. About this time the Silja Line's logo of a seal's head began to appear on the sides of the ships. One of the reasons for this reorganisation was no doubt to enable the partners to meet aggressive competition from the new Viking Line, also a consortium of three Finnish and Swedish shipowners.

By the end of 1972, the *Birger Jarl* must have seemed thoroughly outclassed. Not only did she lack the facilities of the new generation of ferries, but her interiors must have seemed sadly old-fashioned – it was too soon for wooden panelling to assume a period charm. But there were other routes where she could still, perhaps, be viable. In April, 1973 she was sold to a Bore Line subsidiary, the Jakob-Lines for the most northerly ferry service across the Gulf of Bothnia – between Pietarsaari (Jakobstad) and Skellefteå, 63°N. Now called the *Bore Nord* and flying the Finnish flag, she was converted into rather a novel car ferry. An elevator, rather like the tail-lift on a lorry, was attached to the port side of the ship, near the stern. It could lift cars from the quayside up to the after deck. When not in use it was folded away.

2. The *Bore Nord* laid up at Turku in April, 1975 before starting a season of cruises to Visby on the Swedish island of Gotland. *Krzysztof Brzoza.*

The *Bore Nord* spent just one Summer season on the Pietarsaari – Skellefteå route. The following year (1974) the Jakob-Lines chartered her to their parent, the Bore company, for cruises between Turku and Visby on the Swedish island of Gotland. She returned to this service the next Summer, but then had a spell as an accommodation ship off the Norwegian coast.

In October, 1977 she was involved in an exchange deal between Bore and Jakob-Lines. Jakob sold the *Bore Nord* to their parent in part-payment for a slightly bigger and rather younger ship. But Bore Line had no use for their new acquisition and within a few weeks the *Bore Nord* was on the move again, sold on to Minicarriers Ab, associates of Godby Shipping. They planned to convert her to diesel propulsion and to place her in short cruise service between Stockholm and Mariehamn on the Åland Islands. However, nothing happened. The ship lay at Mariehamn and although she was now registered as the *Minisea*, the new name was never painted on her hull.

A year later, in October, 1978, she was sold again – to the Caribbean Shipping Co., Inc. of Panama, which was managed from an office just off Trafalgar Square in London by Gamborg & Co. She was now called the *Baltic Star* and was towed to Turku for refitting. She was chartered to the Ånedin-Linjen. This company's name was a Swedified version of The Onedin Line, the title of a British television series about a

fictional nineteenth-century sailing ship owner, which gained great popularity in several countries. For most of the 'seventies the Ånedin Line had run leisurely 24-hour-long Summertime cruises from Stockholm to Mariehamn and back, using the chartered *Achilleus*, an elderly ex-DFDS ship. They had also experimented with short cruises from Stockholm to Visby, using another chartered Greek-owned vessel, the *Artemis K***. These had not been successful and had been abandoned, but the *Achilleus*'s trips to Mariehamn had proved popular despite the fact that both the Viking and Birka Lines were running similar services with more modern tonnage. One of the owners of the Ånedin Line, Mr Fredrick Sindahl, had a fleet of coaches and brought passengers from around Eastern Sweden to join the ship at the Skeppsbron quay in Stockholm.

By 1978 the *Achilleus* was nearly forty years old and the Caribbean Shipping Company probably bought the *Baltic*

---

***For details of this ship, formerly the *Myconos* of Typaldos Lines, see this author's book Liners & Cruise Ships: Some Notable Smaller Vessels (Carmania Press, 1996).

**4. Now a motor ship, the *Baltic Star* is by 1987 beginning to look rather old-fashioned.** *Krzysztof Brzoza.*

**5. In 1989 she was fitted with a more powerful diesel engine and her appearance was modernised somewhat.**
*Krzysztof Brzoza.*

*Star* with the specific intention that she should replace her. During her refit the *Baltic Star* was given an additional lounge on what had been the after deck. She also assumed the line's rather quirky funnel colours – blue, decorated by white clouds. She entered Ånedin Line's service in 1979. Her first season was not trouble-free but she eventually established herself, inheriting the *Achilleus*'s predominantly middle-aged clientèle. The old ship had borne the legend 'Den Glada Ålands-Baten' along her side (The Happy Åland Boat). The *Baltic Star* did not at first follow suit but years later she began to wear the English words 'Happy Ship'. One of the attractions of her cruises was, of course, the opportunity they offered for duty-free shopping on board.

The *Baltic Star* has not been entirely confined to the Stockholm – Mariehamn run. During her first season, 1979, for instance, she made some 7-day cruises calling at Visby, Ronne, Warnemunde, Gdynia and Riga. Also during that year she had two accidents which could have been very serious indeed. On the 31st May she hit a quay at Mariehamn. In the process, she cut the chains and mooring wires of the famous preserved sailing ship *Pommern* and sank or damaged several pleasure boats. The Lloyd's Casualty Report ascribed the accident to 'a bridge-telegraph misunderstanding' but remarkably no one was

injured and, after being inspected by frogmen, the *Baltic Star* was able, rather shamefacedly, to continue her cruise. Then on the 13th October she stranded in a thick fog while approaching Stockholm. All her passengers were safely removed but the ship remained aground until the following day. She then made her way to the Gotaverken Finnboda yard for examination, where she hit the quay, causing a nasty dent in her stem. Fortunately, in later years she has shewn little sign of these wayward tendencies.

By 1982 the *Baltic Star* was one of the very last steam-driven passenger ships in the Baltic, but her boilers were beginning to be troublesome and it was decided to convert her to diesel propulsion. She went to Frederikshavn to have a B & W Alpha 16-cylinder engine installed. This was not a very powerful unit and the ship's service speed was reduced to just 12¼ knots, but that hardly mattered as the distance between Stockholm and Mariehamn is less than 100 miles. The conversion changed the ship's external appearance since the funnel now became a dummy and a very slender exhaust uptake was installed slightly further aft. This was so discretely done, however, that the by now 'classic' profile seemed hardly to be affected.

Over the years the *Baltic Star*'s owners have spent heavily on improving what is now a very elderly ship. She has had a controllable-pitch propeller fitted in order to

**In recent years the Ånedin Line has added longer cruises to Estonia to its existing programme of cruises to Mariehamn in the Åland Islands. At first the Estonian voyages went to Tallinn but more recently they have headed for the island of Saaremaa.** *Arthur Crook collection.*

# Tallinn

## 4 DAGARS KRYSS fr. 1610:-
Plats i dubbelhytt, halvpension

improve her manoeuvrability and in 1989 she again visited Frederikshavn to be re-engined. The problem with the 1982 engine had apparently been not so much the lack of speed under normal conditions as the fact that it did not have enough oomph to enable the ship to cope with the Baltic ice once the Summer season was over. At the same time the foremast was removed, being replaced by a streamlined signal mast abaft the bridge, and one deck of superstructure was extended forward in order to provide additional cabins and more open deck space. Soon afterwards her funnel lost its decoration of clouds and acquired an arrangement of stripes and the initials CSC (for Caribbean Shipping Company).

In 1988 Gamborg & Co., the managers, became Scandinavian Timber & Marine Services, Ltd., still based in London, but later management of the ship passed to a Stockholm company. The Ånedin Line itself was acquired by Sally Line and, after Sally's collapse, by Effjohn International, parent company of the Silja Line. In the end, however, ownership returned to the Sindahl interests and, according to Arthur Crook, Mr. Sindahl was particularly fond of his ship.

At present the *Baltic Star* continues her regular seasonal service, varied since 1995 by a few trips to Estonia – at first to Tallinn but latterly to the island of Saaremaa. She has also made visits to the Latvian capital, Riga. Fortunately the *Baltic Star* has not been affected by the European Union's ban on the sale of duty free goods on voyages within E.U. waters – exemption has been given for trips to the Åland Islands and, of course, trips to Estonian ports take her outside the restricted area.

# 20

# Covadonga

### Covadonga

Launched as *Monasterio de La Rábida* but completed, 1953, as *Covadonga*. 10,226 gross tons. Length overall: 487 ft. 4 ins. Breadth: 62 ft. 5 ins. Draught: 26 ft. 3½ ins. Single screw. Diesel. Service speed: 16½ knots. Scrapped 1973.

Spain lost most of her empire much sooner than the other European powers. Nevertheless, the main thrust of her westward trade, including migration, was still to South America and the Caribbean basin, to the countries which had once been Spanish possessions and were still Spanish-speaking. The Compañía Trasatlántica Española had several routes to the Caribbean. It did also run ships into U.S. ports, usually New York, but these calls were almost always scheduled as part of long voyages which also took in Cuban and Mexican ports. So the Spanish Line\*\* service to New York was not the kind of quick transatlantic dash favoured by the northern European companies and the Italians.

The Spanish Civil War of 1936-1939 inflicted enormous casualties on the country's merchant fleet. Afterwards, the existing companies resumed their peace-time activities as best they could but in 1943 a government agency set up a new concern, the Empresa Nacional Elcano de la Marina Mercante, with a long-term plan to build 50 ships of several standard types in Spanish yards. Of these, the Type C ships – known as the 'Monasterio' class since initially they were named after Spanish monasteries – were combination cargo and passenger vessels of about 10,000 gross tons. Eventually, they were sold before completion to other operators and were modified to meet the new owners' requirements. The Trasatlántica company bought two of them which had recently been launched as the *Monasterio de Guadalupe* and the *Monasterio de La Rábida* and completed them as the *Guadalupe* and *Covadonga*. Over the years, other 'Monasterio' ships were allocated to the Aznar and Trasmediterránea companies.

Both the *Guadalupe* and the *Covadonga* were built in yards at Bilbao – the *Covadonga* by the Compañía Euskalduna for whom she was yard number 134. Like the rest of her class, she was fitted with a single 10-cylinder Sulzer diesel, in this case the work of the Soc. Española de Construcción Naval, also of Bilbao. It drove a single screw. With five holds giving a total capacity of about 400,000 cubic feet, including some refrigerated space, and

---

\*\*The Trasatlántica company was usually known as the Spanish Line outside Latin countries.

**The Spanish Line's *Covadonga* was a member of the government-inspired 'Monasterio' class. With her long bow and low, streamlined superstructure, she had a stylish appearance.** *Luís Miguel Correia.*

**The *Covadonga* making her maiden arrival at New York, or to be more precise, Hoboken, on the 8th September, 1953.**
*Mark Goldberg collection.*

with deep tanks, she was a considerable cargo-carrier. Consequently, she had a particularly long-bowed look. The superstructure started quite far back and was then long and low, stretching more or less to the stern. This, together with the adoption of kingposts (rather than masts) and a streamlined funnel immediately abaft the bridge, gave the *Covadonga* a rather sleek profile.

She could carry 105 first class passengers and 248 tourist. First class accommodation included five suites, of which three – high up on the boat deck and looking forward over the bow – must have been particularly pleasant (provided you were a good sailor). There were also some single and double cabins with their own verandahs. But in the early 'fifties, even in first class, it was only in a few special cabins such as these that it was thought necessary to provide private facilities. First class passengers did have a swimming pool and also had the benefit of air-conditioning. Tourist class passengers were accommodated in four-berth cabins. It was said at the time

that the public rooms on the *Covadonga* were more Spanish in style than those on her sister, the *Guadalupe*. Both ships had chapels.

The *Covadonga* had been launched as the *Monasterio de La Rábida* in October, 1951 and, as we have seen, was bought by the Trasatlántica company the following year. Completion was not rapid – no doubt in part due to the need to adapt the ship for Trasatlántica's passenger-cargo service. There may have been other reasons too, however. Lloyd's List reported in 1953 that a desperate shortage of materials was slowing down the construction of ships in Spanish yards. Certainly, most of the 'Monasterio' ships seem to have taken four or five years to build.

The *Covadonga* was completed and handed over in mid-1953. There is a slight mystery over her entry into service. Most sources say that her first voyage was a cruise to London in June, 1953 to coincide with the Coronation of Queen Elizabeth II. However, Lloyd's Voyage Records shew her making no such trip and the data on arrivals and departures shews that it was her sister ship, *Guadalupe*, which came into the Pool of London and lay at Butler's Wharf for three days. According to the Voyage Records, *Covadonga* did not sail from Bilbao until the 27th August, when she started her first transatlantic crossing.

That first voyage was not typical. Leaving Bilbao and calling briefly at Santander, Vigo and Lisbon, she then struck out across the Atlantic for New York, before returning straight home to La Coruña, Santander and Bilbao. On most subsequent round trips she would call at Havana and Vera Cruz, either en route to or from New York or as an extension of a direct New York crossing. Occasionally she would call, presumably for cargo, at New Orleans, Mobile, Hampton Roads, Baltimore or Albany, further up the Hudson River from New York. At the European end, she might put in at Madeira, Tenerife, Cadiz, Alicante or Gijon. In July, 1961 she made her only visit to Southampton.

The early years of the Castro government in Cuba must have been a bad time for the Trasatlántica company. The traditional trade links with Spain and with the United States were being severed. The days were soon gone too when droves of American tourists flocked to the country and Carmen Miranda could sing 'How'd you like to spend a weekend in Havana?…You hurry back to your office on Monday, but you won't be the same any more.' And other ties were being cut – it was reported that in 1962 the *Covadonga* carried some of the last Catholic priests to leave Cuba. That October she made her final call at Havana. Henceforth, San Juan in Puerto Rico would often be substituted and there were more direct sailings to and from New York. But as Rodney Mills pointed out in articles in 'Steamboat Bill', the journal of the Steamship Historical Society of America, the figures shew that New York was never a really major passenger port for the Spanish Line.

According to Juan Carlos Diáz Lorenzo, the *Covadonga* acquired a good reputation, especially for the food she served. But through the late '60s and early '70s she was struggling, like so many other liners. Her September, 1971 arrival at New York was her last. Thereafter, she made a few voyages to New Orleans and Houston with calls at San Juan and Vera Cruz and then a few more with Miami as her American terminal port, but when she arrived back at

**First class rooms on the *Covadonga* were furnished in a particularly Spanish style.** *Mark Goldberg collection.*

Bilbao on the 19th January, 1973 she was laid up. The *Guadalupe*, too, was withdrawn and at one time seemed likely to be sold for use as a pilgrim ship. In the end, both ships were sold for scrap. The *Covadonga* made her final, short voyage to Castellon in March, 1973 and was handed over to the breakers. Her career had lasted less than 20 years and her sale, and that of her sister, marked the end of the Trasatlántica company's passenger service between Spain and North America which dated back to 1900. The company itself can trace its origins to a business started in 1850 and still survives as an owner of cargo vessels.

# 21

# Uíge

## Uíge

Completed, 1954. 10,001 gross tons. Length overall: 477 ft. 5 ins. Breadth: 62 ft. 10 ins. Draught: 26 ft. 4 ins. Single screw. Diesel. Service speed: 16 knots. Scrapped 1979.

Like Elder Dempster's *Accra*, which we have already met, the *Uíge* was one of those modest ships which are overshadowed by larger and more glamorous fleetmates but which give great satisfaction to their owners (and their accountants) with years of trouble-free and profitable service. As it happens, both vessels were built for the African trades, on the old colonial routes.

According to Luís Miguel Correia, the Cia. Colonial de Navegação of Lisbon were being pressed by the Portuguese government in the early 1950s to build a large liner to help meet the demand for passages to the country's African possessions. They already had the 21,000-ton *Vera Cruz* and *Santa Maria* under construction for service to

South America and to the Caribbean; now a similar ship should be built for the African routes. The company was not thrilled with the idea. They saw more prospect of profit in a smaller vessel, compatible with the 13,000-ton *Patria* and *Império* which were then the mainstays of the African services. As it happened, the John Cockerill yard at Hoboken in Belgium, who were working on the *Vera Cruz* and the *Santa Maria*, were also booked to produce a freighter for the company. Why not build it as a passenger liner? The point was won and the *Uíge* was the result. The half-joking story was that she was made out of 'off-cuts' from the two larger liners. Shortly afterwards, the rival Cia. Nacional placed an order with Cockerills for a similar ship. (Incidentally, the Cia. Colonial were in the habit of advertising themselves abroad as The Portuguese Line, which must have annoyed the much senior Cia. Nacional.)

The *Uíge*, built in a dry dock, was a modern-looking five-hold motor ship with a well-raked bow and an

**The Portuguese colonial liner *Uíge* leaving her builders' yard at Hoboken in Belgium in 1954.** *Luís Miguel Correia collection.*

The *Uíge* carried her first class passengers in some comfort. Here we see the first class entrance hall and a cabin.
*Luís Miguel Correia collection.*

exceptionally low funnel, to which it was later found necessary to add a short extension pipe. She was given the company's usual livery of grey-green hull and buff funnel with green, white and green bands – similar to the funnel markings of the Holland-America Line, but the colours were of slightly different shades. An 8-cylinder Burmeister & Wain engine, built by Cockerills themselves, drove a single screw. Light alloy was used in the construction of much of the superstructure.

There was accommodation for 78 first class passengers in two de luxe suites and in 2- and 3-berth cabins. All had private facilities. The first class public rooms were a dining room, a lounge and a smoking room. They were very handsomely

furnished in contemporary style. Outside there were facilities for shewing films on the after deck of an evening. There was no permanent swimming pool but, as on so many ships of this type, a temporary one could be placed in one of the hatchways. From a commercial point of view, just as important as the first class passengers were the 493 who could be carried in what was euphemistically called tourist class. They occupied cabins with between 2 and 12 berths. Portuguese citizens were still being encouraged to migrate to the African colonies for some years after it had become clear that the British and Belgian possessions nearby were heading for independence; and indeed the Portuguese retained their colonies rather later than the others. When trouble flared in the Belgian Congo many Belgian citizens fled via the Portuguese territory of Angola and left for Europe on Portuguese ships.

The keel of the new ship was laid on the 19th December, 1952 and she was launched as the *Uíge* on the 23rd January, 1954. She was completed by the end of June and arrived in Lisbon on the 11th July. After loading cargo in Leixões she began her maiden voyage from Lisbon on the 7th August, heading for Luanda which was the destination for much of her traffic. She would usually spend two or three days there working cargo before proceeding to Lobito and Moçamedes. She would then return via the same ports plus Las Palmas and Madeira. (On her maiden voyage, and occasionally later, she made an additional call at the island of São Tomé.) At times in the late 'fifties the demand for passages to Angola was such that one of the big 21,000-tonners would have to be brought in for some voyages to Luanda. It was in order to release the *Santa Maria* for this service that in July, 1958 the *Uíge* made her one and only run on the South American route, to Rio de Janeiro and Santos. Otherwise she was confined almost entirely to the west coast of Africa run and it was only in June, 1975, almost at the end of her

The *Uíge* laid up at Lisbon some time before she was scrapped in 1979. Until the disintegration of the Portuguese African empire she had been a quietly successful ship. *Luís Miguel Correia.*

career, that she was used on the longer African route, beyond Luanda and round the Cape to Beira.

Eventually, trouble began to stir in Portuguese Africa and increasingly the liners of the Colonial and Nacional companies were used to carry troops. In 1964, the *Uíge* made her first trooping voyage to Bissao in Guinea and over the next few years these became quite frequent. She also carried troops to and from Luanda.

Other things were changing too, and a new, more left-wing government imposed a gradual re-organisation on the Portuguese shipping industry. In February, 1974 the Cia. Colonial was merged with the Empresa Insulana to form the CTM Cia. Portuguesa de Transportes Marítimos). Colonial's subtle funnel colours were painted over, superseded by a rather brash orange-red with blue, yellow and blue bands. At the time, the *Uíge* was already

being used by the Insulana company for three voyages on their route to Madeira and the Azores. The following year she was used by the government in connection with the Portuguese withdrawal from the newly-independent Cape Verde islands.

With the Empire gone and the Portuguese passenger fleet being run down as rapidly as those of so many other nations, it was inevitable that the *Uíge*'s career should be cut short. She was laid up at Lisbon in January, 1976, remaining idle until March, 1979 when she was scrapped locally. Recently, Luís Miguel Correia shewed me a model of her in a marvellous room, full of models, in the Maritime Museum at Lisbon. It was quite clear, despite that low funnel, that the *Uíge* had been a very attractive ship.

# 22

# Meteor

### *Meteor / Zephiros / Neptune*

Completed 1955 as *Meteor*. 2,856 gross tons. Length overall: 296 ft. 8 ins. Breadth: 45 ft. 1 ins. Draught: 16 ft. 0³/₄ ins. Single screw. Diesel. Service speed: 18 knots. Became *Zephiros* (1971) and *Neptune* (1971). 2,402 gross tons.

Norway has been involved in the cruise business since the very early days. As often as not it was to see the fjords and the North Cape that the early British and German cruise ships took their passengers. And Norwegian companies, too, were not slow to recognise the tourist potential of their coast. The Hurtigruten, the regular passenger/cargo service which provides a link with the remote communities of Northern Norway, began also to be marketed as a tourist attraction. Two of the concerns involved in the Hurtigruten, the Bergen Line and Nordenfjeldske, went further and acquired vessels specifically for cruising.

Before the Second World War the Bergen company (Det Bergenske Dampskibsselskab) had two famous cruise ships – the *Meteor*, a former Hamburg America Line 'cruising-yacht' which they had bought in 1921; and the *Stella Polaris* which was one of the most exclusive cruise ships of her time, the equivalent of to-day's Sea Goddess and Seabourn vessels. After the War the company restored the *Stella Polaris* and brought her back into service. But the market for her luxurious, expensive cruises was diminished and such passengers as there were preferred ships with more modern facilities. So, in 1951, the *Stella Polaris* was sold to Swedish buyers.

Thereafter, the Bergen Line's cruising activities were rather different. The *Venus*, a notable North Sea passenger ferry, was transferred in the slack Winter months to a more southerly scheduled service between Britain and Madeira, at first from Plymouth but later from Southampton. Her voyages could be sold as round-trip cruises to the sun, just as the Yeoward, Aznar and Fred. Olsen services to the Canaries were for many years. Although she was essentially a ferry and there could be no disguising the fact that many of her cabins were tiny, the *Venus* served very well as a cruise ship and she became very popular, particularly after being fitted with stabilisers.

In December, 1952 the company placed an order with the Aalborg Vaerft A/S for a new cruise ship which could also serve as a relief vessel for the Hurtigruten and the North Sea ferry services. Aalborg Vaerft was the Danish yard which had recently delivered three 2,100-ton vessels for the Hurtigruten. Two of them belonged to the Bergen Line. The new ship, although slightly larger, would be similar. Loyalists hoping for another *Stella Polaris* may have been disappointed. That old favourite had been a

**Although mainly used as a comfortable small cruise ship, the *Meteor* could be easily converted for a more workaday role in the Bergen Line's North Sea ferry service or on the Coastal Express.** *John G. Callis, Ambrose Greenway collection.*

'cruising yacht' with a clipper bow and a tall, elegantly raked steamship funnel (although she was in fact a motor ship). She had the looks of a big private yacht of the kind which royalty and the super-rich had sometimes given themselves as a present in more affluent days. The new ship, for which the name *Meteor* was revived, was smaller and had a more functional appearance. She seems, in fact, to have been shaped by the requirements of the Hurtigruten. Nevertheless, she was a trim-looking vessel in her cruising livery of a white hull and a buff funnel instead the usual Bergen Line black (although still with the famous three widely-spaced white bands).**

A 9-cylinder turbo-charged Burmeister & Wain diesel engine drove a single controllable-pitch propeller. Deep in the hull was a cargo hold, refrigerated for the carriage of fish on Hurtigruten voyages. The ship was partly riveted, partly welded and aluminium was used in the construction of her superstructure. As a Hurtigruten ship the *Meteor* could carry 90 first class passengers (in a cabin de luxe, two other 'special cabins' and a selection of single- and double-berth cabins, all with private facilities). Up to 110 second class passengers could be accommodated in 2-, 3-, 4- and 6-berth cabins. Also, as always on the Hurtigruten, there would be other passengers merely using the ship as a 'local bus' between nearby ports.

Arrangements for the rapid conversion of the ship for her cruising role were ingenious. The first class dining room, for instance, could be extended simply by pulling back a partition, thus taking in the adjacent second class lounge. The result was an extremely spacious dining room complete with its own bar and dance floor. Other public rooms when the ship was in cruising mode were a lounge, a smoke room, a bar and a verandah. (The country's laws at the time forbad opening bars on Norwegian ships when they were in coastal waters, so they were always closed when the *Meteor* was in Hurtigruten service.) When she was cruising she had a ship's shop and a hairdressing salon. Hurtigruten passengers on the other hand, scored over the pampered cruisers in two respects, since on the coastal route a post office and a hospital were available, part of the service which the government-subsidised Hurtigruten offered to the more isolated inhabitants of the North. As a cruise ship the *Meteor* could carry up to 160 passengers in a single class which included some of the 2-berth cabins of the erstwhile second class. The rest of the second class cabins were closed off. All the *Meteor* lacked as a cruise ship was a swimming pool. Otherwise she was well suited to the role – she was comfortable (even if some of the cabins were a little on the small side), the food was notably good and the service was willing – which must have been a pleasant change in times which were still afflicted by post-War grumpiness.

The *Meteor* was launched on the 5th May, 1954 and was completed in January 1955. On trials she achieved a speed of 18$\frac{1}{2}$ knots, the requirements of the cruising trade dictating that she should have a more powerful engine and higher speed than the regular Hurtigruten ships. She set off on her first Hurtigruten voyage on the 22nd January, 1955. From Bergen to Kirkenes, in the Far North, and back is a round trip of 2,500 miles and with up to 40 calls en route it was in 1955 scheduled to take 13 days, The

*Meteor* was due to start her first season of cruising that Summer, but in the event she had to be taken off the Hurtigruten sooner than expected. Late in March the *Venus* was blown ashore by gale force winds in Plymouth Sound and was only refloated, in a highly damaged state, after several anxious days. As soon as possible the *Meteor* was sent to Plymouth to take over the last two trips of the *Venus*'s Madeira season. Then she made her debut on the ferry service from Bergen to the Tyne before, in June, starting a programme of cruises out of Bergen to the Baltic, the North Cape and Spitzbergen. In the Autumn she started a stint on the Bergen - Tyne and Bergen - Rotterdam ferry routes.

So, for a few years, a pattern was established: Autumn and Winter on the Hurtigruten or the North Sea ferry routes, with the rest of the year spent cruising from Bergen and from either Harwich or Dover, including one long trip out to the Mediterranean and Black Sea which could be marketed in two separate three-week sections. There might also be a round-Scotland cruise from Leith or Ardrossan. After 1958, however, the Hurtigruten and the North Sea routes, for which the *Meteor* had been partly designed, no longer needed her and she was used entirely for cruising, spending the Winter months in lay-up. Then, from 1960 onwards, new Winter employment was found for her, cruising the Caribbean out of St. Thomas and San Juan. In 1960 and 1961 she made two long visits to her builders' yard at Aalborg to be turned into a full-time cruise ship.

For the next decade there was little variation in the *Meteor*'s programme – Winter in the Caribbean, followed by a brief visit to the Mediterranean, a few British Isles cruises (one often under charter to The National Trust for Scotland), a season of northern cruises out of Bergen, a rather longer return to the Mediterranean and then back to the Caribbean. In 1970, however, change came – in two ways. Ownership of the vessel was transferred to a new company, Meteor Cruises A/S in which the Bergen Line had an interest, but now in partnership with another Bergen shipping firm, Rolf Wigand. And she was withdrawn from the European market – from now onwards she would spend the Summer months cruising to Alaska out of Vancouver.

It was during her second Alaskan season that, on the 22nd May, 1971, the *Meteor* met disaster in a particularly nasty way. When she was just 60 miles away from Vancouver, fire broke out in the crew's quarters. It spread with terrible rapidity. All the passengers were herded into lifeboats and were picked up by the ferry *Malaspina*, but 32 crew were trapped and died. The captain and some of the crew remained on board and on the second attempt brought the fire under control, helped by tugs and Coast Guard cutters. On the 23rd, listing but under her own power, the *Meteor* limped into Vancouver. The police cordoned off the area round her and eventually she was taken to the Burrard shipyard. Amidst a swirl of allegations and Inquiries the *Meteor* lay at Vancouver for some months. Eventually she was sold.

---

**I have, though, seen one photograph of the ship with a black funnel.

**After her tragic fire off the coast of British Columbia in May, 1971, the *Meteor* is sprayed by Canadian Coast Guard vessels.** *Laurence Dunn collection.*

That was not the end of the Bergen Line's involvement in the cruise business, however. They were one of the founding partners in the, ultimately, hugely influential Royal Viking Line. A few years ago I was shewn round the *Royal Viking Sun*, then the most highly-rated cruise ship in the World. I was delighted to see that, although the Royal Viking Line had by then become part of the Kloster group and the Bergen Line itself had been dismembered, the Bergen connection had not been forgotten. A magnificent observation lounge was named after the *Stella Polaris* and elsewhere one came across a beautiful model of the *Venus*.

The buyers of the *Meteor* were Greek – Epirotiki Lines (the Epirotiki Steam Navigation Co. 'George Potamianos' S.A.). Run by the Potamianos family who can trace their shipping activities back to 1833, Epirotiki came into prominence in the early 1950s when they were amongst the pioneers of Greek island cruising. Indeed, their *Semiramis* (originally Elder Dempster's African coastal liner *Calabar*) could lay claim to being the very first vessel specifically devoted to that trade. In the mid-'sixties Epirotiki began an ambitious expansion with newer, rather bigger ships, still second-hand but refurbished to quite a high standard. They were soon cruising far beyond the Greek islands.

When, in late 1971, Epirotiki bought the *Meteor*, they took her 'as is'. The crew accommodation in the fore part of the ship had been utterly gutted by the fire and the passenger quarters further aft were badly damaged by smoke and water. The ship sailed from Vancouver on the 20th October under the name *Zephiros* and flying the Greek flag. She arrived in Piraeus 30 days later. She was repaired and by April, 1972 was ready for service, now as the *Neptune*. (Herein lies confusion – the ship appears in Lloyd's Register as *Neptune*, is marketed under that name and carries it on her bow; but the Greek letters on her stern spell out the name *Poseidon*. Neptune (or rather, Neptunus) was the Roman name for the god of the sea; to the Greeks he was Poseidon. Similarly, Epirotiki's *Jupiter* bore the name *Zeus* an her stern.)

*Neptune*'s hull was painted the characteristic Epirotiki fawn and her blue funnel carried their quatrefoil insignia**. In a typically Greek reconstruction, the superstructure was extended fore and aft and a swimming pool was installed. Internally, the ship was extensively refurnished by Maurice Bailey, a fashionable designer of the day who had already worked on several of the company's vessels, The Epirotiki ships became well-known for their modern art-works on classical themes. As restored, the *Neptune* could accommodate up to 213 single-class passengers in 1-, 2-, and 3-berth cabins, all with private facilities.

---

**Actually a Byzantine cross.

**Described by her owners, Epirotiki Lines, as 'a jewel among cruise ships', the *Neptune* is seen here at Piraeus in April, 1977.**
*Ambrose Greenway.*

*Neptune*'s career with Epirotiki has been varied, to say the least. At first, in 1972, she ran 7-day cruises out of Piraeus, round the islands of the southern Aegean and often on to Turkish ports. The following year she was making 7-day cruises from Nice to Venice. Later she spent her Summers in 3- and 4-day cruise service round the islands and then in 1979 she was again running 7-day cruises out of Venice. Her Winters were at first spent in the Caribbean, cruising out of San Juan but by the late '70s she had moved on to Red Sea cruises from Suez. Epirotiki have been greatly given to chartering their ships out to other operators and *Neptune* did her share of this work in the 1980s, appearing in Spanish and Portuguese ports, round Northern Europe, in the Red Sea and in the Indian Ocean. She visited several British ports in 1988, 1989 and 1990. By the early '90s, however, she was mainly running for her owners in the Aegean.

A few years earlier she had been transferred within the Epirotiki group to a concern called the Hellenic Company for Mediterranean Cruises but this was a purely financial move and did not affect her operations or her funnel colours. A more obvious change was that in 1988 she was given a fairly major refit. Her interiors were refurbished and her funnel was re-shaped and acquired a rather unsightly smoke deflector. She still had that foursquare 1950s look, however, and was indeed by now a fairly elderly ship, one of the few without stabilisers still operating in the cruise market.

In the mid-1990s, with the massive cruise groups which had hitherto concentrated on the Caribbean now eyeing the Mediterranean, the family-owned Greek lines began to look vulnerable. Epirotiki flirted with Klosters and then even got as far as reaching an agreement which gave the giant Carnival Cruise Lines group a substantial stake. However, this alliance rapidly fell apart and, instead, Epirotiki merged the major part of their operations with another Greek firm which seemed endangered, Sun Lines. The new, combined group started business under the name Royal Olympic Cruises in December, 1995.

The *Neptune* was not included in the deal. Along with most of Epirotiki's other smaller and older ships she was transferred to a new company, Hermes Cruises (now called Olympic Short Cruises) which concentrates on day cruises and other short trips. In fact, Epirotiki had not used her during 1995 and she remained in lay-up. Word is, however, that in 1999 she is acting in a static mode, being let out for weddings and other receptions – rather a comedown after her long career as quite a notable cruise ship.

**Confusingly, the *Neptune* bears the Greek name *Poseidon* on her stern.** *Peter Newall.*

# 23
# Jedinstvo

### *Jedinstvo / Ambasador / Aquanaut Ambasador / Ambasador 1*

Completed, 1958. 2,637 gross tons. Length overall: 295 ft. 6 ins. Breadth: 42 ft. 10 ins. Draught: 15 ft. 5¾ ins. Twin screw. Diesel. Service speed: 17½ knots. Became *Ambasador* (1978), *Aquanaut Ambasador* (1989), *Ambasador 1* (1990).

It was not only the Greeks who realised in the 1950s that, with the tourist industry beginning to boom, they had potential for cruising along their coasts and among their islands. Further up the Adriatic, the Yugoslavs, too, acquired some small cruise ships which could work their way along the rugged coastline and take their passengers to often quite tiny ports. In Greece, although the government gave encouragement and even provided several new ships, the cruise business was run by individual shipowners, usually family concerns. By contrast, in Communist Yugoslavia it was state-owned. As a result, whereas the early Greek cruise fleet was a diverse assembly of often elderly second hand vessels, the Yugoslav cruise ships came in batches from the state shipyards.

As in Norway and Turkey, regular coastal passenger/cargo ship services had long played an important role in the national transport system. The new cruise business was really an extension of these services which were operated by Jadranska Linijska Plovidba,

usually known as Jadrolinija and one of the country's several state-owned shipping companies. This concern seems to have been running cruises from about 1953 onwards but it was between 1956 and 1958, with the introduction of three new 2,500-ton vessels, that it went into business in earnest.

The first two of this new trio, the *Jugoslavija* and the *Jadran*, were still intended for regular scheduled service and they had accommodation not only for first and tourist passengers but also for considerable numbers of deck passengers. But they were a cut above the usual coastal vessels – the *Jadran*, for instance, had a swimming pool – and they sailed out of Venice, from whence their round voyages could be sold as tourist trips. The *Jadran*, indeed, having progressed down the Yugoslav coast would then head for the Greek ports of Corfu and Piraeus before returning. In between times, they were available for pure cruising. The third ship the *Jedinstvo*, was intended from the outset as a full-time cruise ship, but with a little cargo space.

She differed from her near-sisters in a number of ways but, most importantly, she was a one-class ship. She, too, had a swimming pool on the boat deck. Her accommodation was fully air-conditioned but only a limited number of her cabins were given full facilities. Most of them contained two berths and the ship had a total passenger capacity of 221. Public rooms were

**The *Jedinstvo* was built for Jadrolinija especially for cruising along the Yugoslav coast.** *Laurence Dunn collection.*

In the 1980s the ship, now called *Ambasador*, was owned by a Yugoslav travel agency. She is seen here at Valletta.
*Laurence Dunn collection.*

pleasant without being lavish. She was painted white overall except for Jadrolinija's funnel markings of narrow black top and dark red star.

Like her two companions the *Jedinstvo* was built at Split by Brodogradiliste "Split" for whom she was yard number 132. They completed her in January, 1958. Her hull was part-welded and she was given two Sulzer 8-cylinder diesel engines which had been built by the Werkspoor company of Amsterdam. She was registered at Rijeka.

She was mainly based at Venice from where she operated Adriatic and Greek island cruises under charter to Yugotours and some German tour operators. The Yugoslav sisters were, in fact, among the very first cruise ships to be marketed in Germany after the War. The *Jedinstvo* seems to have proved popular with her German passengers. Rainer Tiemann took a cruise on her in 1962 and remembers open-air lectures in the evenings under the Mediterranean sky. He liked the ship sufficiently to commission an attractive painting of her, many years later – this despite the fact that he found the portions at mealtimes less than satisfying to a youthful appetite. The painting shews the ship making her way through the Lagoon at Venice. It was there that in August, 1959 she had collided with a small Italian stone-carrier. The Italian ship had to be beached to prevent her from sinking but damage to the *Jedinstvo* was slight and she was able to proceed. Then in 1962 she collided at Rhodes with the Typaldos Line's *Adriatiki*, but again she was able to continue her cruise.

In 1965 Jadrolinija introduced two bigger and altogether superior ships, the *Dalmacija* and *Istra*. They were also based at Venice but were operated on a longer route which took them on a circuit of the Eastern Mediterranean. They were also used for long-distance cruising to such areas as South America, the Caribbean and the Baltic. Between 1968 and 1971 the *Jedinstvo* found Winter employment under charter to the Grimaldi group's Siosa Line, operating fly-cruises from Tenerife down the West African coast. But by the mid-'seventies she and her two sisters were no longer considered suitable for the international cruise market. The *Jugoslavija* was sold in 1973 and eventually became Epirotiki's day-cruiser *Hermes*. The *Jadran* was sold for use as a floating restaurant at Toronto where she remains to this day. For a while Jadrolinija kept the *Jedinstvo* but in 1978 they disposed of her to a travel firm, again state-owned, the Atlas Jugoslavenska Putnicka Agecija of Dubrovnik.

Atlas re-named her *Ambasador* – note the spelling – and had her refitted at Split. They often used her for 7-day '1,000 Island Cruises' (Dubrovnik – Korcula – Hvar – Sibenik – Venice – Opatija – Rijeka –Kornati – Kotor – Dubrovnik). From time to time, however, she was seen elsewhere – in Genoa and Istanbul, for instance – and she spent the Winter of 1987-8 in the Caribbean. It is said that under Atlas ownership she was less well-maintained than she had been in her early days with Jadrolinija and that she had a disconcerting list. However, in 1985 she was 'taken

**The *Ambasador 1*, as she became, has most recently been used for cruises round the Galapagos islands.**
*Marion J. Browning.*

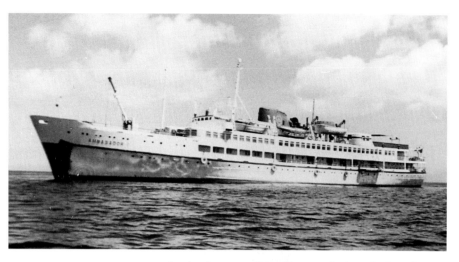

in hand' and refitted in readiness for a charter to Salén-Lindblad, the long-distance expedition cruise operators. She now accommodated just 120 passengers. For Salén-Lindblad she cruised in the Indian Ocean, the Red Sea and elsewhere. The arrangement was sufficiently successful for the two companies, in 1987, to sign a preliminary contract with the 3 Maj yard, also Yugoslavian, for a somewhat larger replacement. The deal fell through.

In 1988 Atlas sold the *Ambasador* for $1.8 million to a company called Dive & Sail Holidays Ltd. of Fort Lauderdale who in the following year registered her under the Panamanian flag and called her *Aquanaut Ambasador*. The new enterprise was known as the Aquanaut Cruise Line and was also operating two small vessels in the Caribbean. There have been several attempts to establish a niche market for water sports cruises, notably with the *Ocean Spirit*, formerly the pioneer Florida cruise vessel *Sunward*, which was being operated in this way at about the same time. None of these ventures seem to have been successful. In the event, the *Aquanaut Ambasador* was not used for water sports cruises but instead, in the Summer of 1989, was running orthodox cruises down the Yugoslav coast. Arthur Crook was on board during one of these. She had been given what he calls 'a cosmetic uplift', but he was not impressed. 'The food was good (Italian) but the accommodation was terrible. We had to move cabin several times due to leaking plumbing. However, the scenery made up for these shortcomings.' This phase of the ship's career did not last long as Dive and Sail Holidays failed within months and the ship was laid up in a Yugoslav port, for sale.

The next owners were a company called Adriatic Cruises Ltd. They re-named the ship *Ambasador 1* and had her refurbished at the Zadar yard. A Jadrolinija-like star appeared on her funnel, but now in a circle, and the old weekly '1,000 Island cruises' out of Dubrovnik were resurrected – but now they were '1,200 Island cruises'. There were also some longer Mediterranean jaunts. In the summer of 1991 the *Ambasador 1* was chartered for some cruises round the coasts of the British Isles. A well-known cruise guide gave her the second lowest rating of any cruise ship and before long she was laid up at Piraeus, still under the Panamanian flag.

There she languished for many months, now in the ownership of New York Greeks, Ionian Transport Inc. Finally, in 1993 gainful employment was found for her. She was chartered to the Galapagos Tourist Corporation as a replacement for their *Bucaneer* ( ex-*St. Ninian*) which

was to be broken up. Lloyd's noted the *Ambasador 1* sailing westward through the Panama Canal on the 19th July, 1993. She was on her way to Guayaquil and a new career carrying tourists around the Galapagos Islands. Now flying the Ecuadorian flag, she carried a maximum of 86 passengers – because of the delicate nature of the environment in the islands the number of tourists allowed to visit them is very strictly limited. Marion Browning made the trip in 1997 and says that the *Ambasador 1* was 'ideal for leisurely cruising around the islands. The engineers were all Croatian as they were familiar with this older Yugoslav ship – the engine room looked immaculate.' The rest of the crew was local, but with Greek officers.

As this is written in 1999, the *Ambasador 1* continues in cruise service around the Galapagos Islands. She has been partly block-booked by Marine Expeditions, the specialist cruise operators, who market her under the name *Marine Ambassador*, although to her other passengers and to Lloyd's Register she remains *Ambasador 1*.

**A near-sister, the *Jadran* is now a floating restaurant in Toronto.** *Bill Appleton.*

# 24

## INTERLUDE
# Farewell to the Fanny Duck

One of the most frustrating things about writing about ships which are still remembered is that inevitably, once the die is cast and the book is published, you hear from people whose recollections would have breathed extra life into some of the chapters. Of all the vessels covered in my book Liners & Cruise Ships, the one which has prompted the greatest crop of memories has been the *Nova Scotia* which later became the *Francis Drake*.

It should, perhaps, be explained that the *Nova Scotia* started life in 1947 as one of a pair of 7,000-ton cargo-passenger liners built for the Furness-Warren Line's Liverpool – St. John's – Halifax – Boston service. She and her sister ship, the *Newfoundland*, were solid, unpretentious vessels and they plodded on until 1962 when they became early victims of the competition from the new jet aeroplanes. Donald Stoltenberg, the American artist whose painting of the *Nova Scotia* adorns the rear cover of this book, knew them both. From his home in Boston, he watched their comings and goings; and he sailed on the *Newfoundland*. 'They were not luxurious, but they were very comfortable and had a nice atmosphere. Of course, because they called at St. John's and Halifax before reaching Boston and because they were as much cargo

ships as passenger liners, they could be late in arriving. But then, their first class fares were cheaper than those on the express liners to New York. At the end, it was very sad – when they went, nobody took any notice of the departure of such familiar ships; there was not even a mention in the local press. They just slipped away.'

They were quickly bought by the Australian firm of H. C. Sleigh, Ltd. who registered them in the name of the Dominion Navigation Company, called them *Francis Drake* and *George Anson* and had them converted for a new passenger-cargo service between Australia and the Far East. These quiet, unglamorous liners proceeded to arouse as much affection and loyalty as many of the big, exciting and luxurious floating palaces.

Shortly after Liners & Cruise Ships was published I received a fax from Dr. John McMichan, an Australian now resident in the United States. He wrote. 'The book is even more significant for my wife, Jan, and myself as it contains one of the few written accounts of the *Francis Drake*. Both of us travelled on her, we met on her, we had our first date on her and both of us were members of the ship's company, but not at the same time.'

He continues: 'Following her transfer to the Dominion

**Seen at Sydney in 1965 in the new colours of the Dominion Far East Line, the *Francis Drake* was a handy-sized passenger-cargo liner.** *Ambrose Greenway.*

Typhoons were one of the hazards faced by ships on the Australia – Far East run.
*Photograph: John Macdonald; pressure recording: John and Jan McMichan collection.*

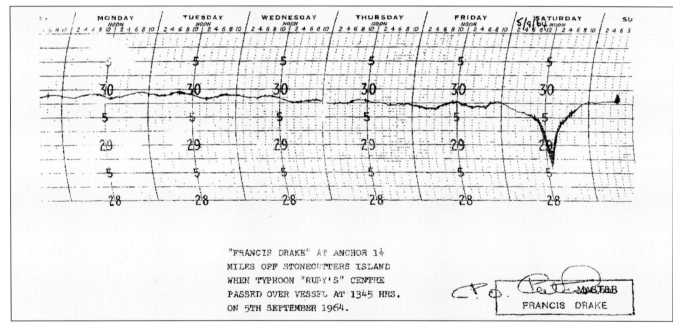

"FRANCIS DRAKE" AT ANCHOR 1¼ MILES OFF STONECUTTERS ISLAND WHEN TYPHOON "RUBY'S" CENTRE PASSED OVER VESSEL AT 1345 HRS. ON 5TH SEPTEMBER 1964.

FRANCIS DRAKE

Line the *Francis Drake* made a few voyages carrying only a doctor in the medical department. Then, in September, 1963, following a position as Nursing Sister with P & O on board the *Himalaya* and *Arcadia*, my wife joined the 'Fanny Duck' (as the *Francis Drake* was affectionately known) as Nurse / Librarian / Nanny. Her second voyage left Melbourne on the 25th November, 1963 and I was on board as a passenger. In the den of our home we have a photo of the ship taken by a friend, as she leaves Station Pier in Melbourne. Clearly visible are my wife, in uniform, and myself. We had not met at that stage. The voyage was of ten weeks' duration and included a ten-day drydocking in Kowloon, Hong Kong.

'In the following years I finished my medical studies and Jan stayed with the *Francis Drake*, making five round trips each year. Your book recounts the encounter with Typhoon 'Ruby' in September, 1964. I am sending a copy of the original pressure recording as the storm passed over the ship. It is signed by the Master, Captain G. Oliver Gatehouse. Jan was on board for the duration.

'In 1969, three years after I had graduated from medical school, I was about to set off for London to undertake studies in surgery, when I found I had three months to fill in. I called H. C. Sleigh and obtained the position as ship's doctor on the *Francis Drake*. However, Jan had already signed off and I sailed with another nurse! It was a wonderful voyage, full of medical adventures. Once again, the ship was dry-docked in Hung Hom Bay in Kowloon and I was able to walk under her keel! On my return to Melbourne the company offered me a permanent position. I was sorely tempted but turned it down in favour of continuing my surgical studies. I often wonder what would have happened to my career if I had accepted. I returned from Britain in 1971 and Jan and I married in 1974.'

The McMichans have vivid memories of their times on this very pleasant intermediate liner, 'a ship which carried about 100 passengers, deck officers who were mainly of British descent, and a crew of Hong Kong Chinese.' They recall 'the Forward Lounge of wood-panelled walls, leather armchairs and couches, a non-functioning fireplace, a small library and afternoon tea served from a silver tea service. The Dining Room, which you entered via a bifurcated staircase, had a central dance floor with a small bandstand and portholes on each side of the room which frequently descended beneath the waves as the ship rolled heavily through the swells of the South China Sea.' (She was not stabilised.) ' After dinner you took coffee and liqueurs in the Smoking Room while the Dining Room was prepared for the evening's entertainment. There were formal nights of black ties, long gowns and dancing among colourful streamers and balloons; and informal nights with horse racing, quizzes, slide and music shows provided by the crew and a passenger talent show. You would end with a late night drink in the 'Snake Pit', a bar way aft below decks.'

There were also 'tropical barbecues on deck, with food cooked on open fires. The 'Barber Shop' was on deck, where a seated passenger would be surrounded by a white table cloth and tended by one of the cabin stewards. There might be a late-afternoon game of deck golf, passengers vs. officers. There was a camaraderie among passengers and crew.'

'Keeping the passengers entertained during such a long voyage was one of my main concerns.' according to John Macdonald, at one time Purser on the *Francis Drake*, who also contacted me following the publication of Liners & Cruise Ships. 'One of my innovations was a Hawaiian 'Lovou' – an informal meal held out on the after deck, which we decorated with palm fronds. After the first one, I was horrified to learn that we had paid $1 per frond at the previous port.

'Hong Kong crews are well-known for smuggling and every voyage into Australia we were inundated with customs officers – usually at every port and often ripping the same areas to bits on each occasion, particularly the wooden panelling in the Lounge. My attitude to the crew in my own department was that if it was watches, transistors or the like, that was between them and the customs. However, I made it quite clear that I would not tolerate drugs of any sort and if they were found with them, their job was gone. Nevertheless, on one voyage in Sydney I was very tempted to re-think my attitude on watches. I went to bed and woke up wondering what on earth was ticking. On investigation I found that my cabin steward had decided that I would not be searched and had placed his entire stock of watches under my mattress. In fact, I was often searched, as was every other member of the complement, with the possible exception of the Master. Fortunately, on this occasion it did not occur but I can assure you that they were removed very swiftly once

I got hold of the steward in the morning.

'In some ports out east you have to be prepared to donate quite large quantities of cigarettes and spirits, otherwise you will suffer very long delays in obtaining the necessary clearances to enter port. Many of our passengers could not believe what they were seeing and often asked why we gave in to their demands. We had to point out that if they wished to get ashore and not to be left out at anchor while cargo was unloaded into barges, then we had to comply.'

John Macdonald also remembers that Sir Hamilton Sleigh, chairman of H. C. Sleigh, Ltd., took a very personal interest in his company's two passenger ships. There was, for instance, the episode when they started using metal polymer polish on the passenger decks of the *Francis Drake*. It made an enormous difference to the appearance of the ship – so much so that when they were moored next to the rival *Aramac* of the Eastern & Australian Steamship Company, passengers were remarking how very much cleaner the *Francis Drake* was. (In fact, the two ships were probably as clean as each other.) Unfortunately, the polish had to be applied with an extremely expensive machine. During the voyage, word reached John Macdonald that Sir Hamilton was furious at the amount of money he had spent. When they arrived back at Melbourne, Sir Hamilton came on board for his usual inspection, together with various company officials. Nothing was said until the very end of the visit, when Sir Hamilton said, 'You will leave this ship.' That, it seemed, was the end of a promising career – but the great man added, 'You will go to the *George Anson*' (the sister ship) 'and do the same for her.'

The McMichans remember the industrial unrest among the dockers in Australian ports which interfered with cargo-handling and delayed departures. In any case, competition from the jet aeroplane and the container ship was bringing to an end the era of the combination passenger-cargo liner.

'It was a sad day for me,' John McMichan recalls, 'when in 1971, with a large group of friends of the *Francis Drake*, I stood at the point where the Yarra River empties into Port Philip Bay in Melbourne. The *Francis Drake*, fully decked out in flags and buntings, sailed in front of me for the last time. In response to the hooting of our car horns, she replied with three deep blasts from her whistle. That was the last I saw of a ship that meant, and still means, a lot to both Jan and myself.

'Years later, I set out to find the model of the ship which used to sit in the entrance foyer of the H. C. Sleigh Building in Melbourne. I recently stumbled on it, a gift from the Sleigh family appropriately housed in a maritime museum in Melbourne. However, we have numerous other memorabilia of the ship gathered by my wife and myself during our time on board.'

The *Francis Drake* had been completed in 1947 as the *Nova Scotia* by Vickers-Armstrongs, Walker-on-Tyne. 7,438 gross tons. Length overall: 440 ft. 6 ins. Breadth: 61 ft. 2 ins. Draught: 25 ft. 6 ins. Single-screw. Geared turbines. Service speed: 15 knots. Became *Francis Drake*, 1962. Scrapped, 1971.

# 25

# St. Helena

### *Northland Prince / St. Helena / Avalon / Indocéanique*

Completed 1963 as *Northland Prince*. 3,150 gross tons. Length overall: 329 ft. 0 ins. Breadth: 48 ft. 0 ins. Draught: 18 ft. 0³/₄ ins. Single screw. Diesel. Service speed: 16 knots. Became *St. Helena* (1977), *St. Helena Island* (1989), *Avalon* (1991). *Indocéanique* (1994). Scrapped 1996.

When, in 1977, a small Cornish company called Curnow Shipping, Ltd., won the government contract to run the mail, passenger and cargo service from Britain to St Helena and Ascension and on to Cape Town, there must have been many people in the shipping industry who had to turn to their reference books to discover who Curnow were. The company had, in fact, been founded a few years earlier by Andrew Bell and its main activity had hitherto been the transport of building materials to West Africa using small, chartered vessels. Now, however, the directors saw their opportunity to move into a bigger league.

The opening occurred because the Union-Castle Line and their South African associates, Safmarine, were abandoning their famous express mail service from Southampton to Cape Town. On some of these sailings a diversion had been made to the minute British island of St Helena, way out in the South Atlantic. Without an airport, St Helena has to rely on sea transport for its supplies and for a passenger link not only with Britain but also with South Africa. In addition, a connexion with Ascension, 800 miles to the north-west, is important since many St Helenians find work on that island.

The British government was forced to put the service out to tender and, eventually, Curnow Shipping won the contract because they had managed to locate just about the only suitable small passenger-cargo ship then available. The search had not been easy. They had looked at no less than 27 vessels, including three belonging to the Tirrenia Line and also the former *Koolama* (the 'Koolamity' as she was sometimes unkindly known), once of the State Shipping Service of Western Australia. The quest ended, though, when a neighbour of Andrew Bell's, newly returned from a trip to Canada, mentioned that, while there, he had travelled on a coastal ship which had since been laid up at Vancouver. She proved to be the *Northland Prince*.

She had been conceived by Canadians but by the time her keel was laid she already had a Dutch step-parent. In

**The *Northland Prince* was built for a subsidised passenger and cargo service from Vancouver to the ports up the sparsely populated coast of British Columbia.** *John D. Henderson.*

**Refitted to maintain the link between Britain and her South Atlantic possessions, the former *Northland Prince*, now called *St. Helena*, acquired a streamlined signal mast.** *Mike Lennon.*

1962 the well-known Rotterdam shipping firm of Phs. Van Ommeren took a stake in the Northland Navigation Company, based in Vancouver, and later they gained control. Northland and a predecessor company had been operating small ships along the coast of British Columbia since 1942. The *Northland Prince* was to be a bigger and altogether superior vessel, carrying passengers and cargo from Vancouver up the Inside Passage to Stewart, at 55°N the northernmost port in British Columbia. Supported by a government subsidy, she was to maintain a regular weekly service – six-day round trips with eight calls in the northward direction and three on the return leg.

The service was often compared to the Norwegian coastal express and, indeed, the purpose was similar. Passengers and supplies were carried to small and, in some cases, otherwise isolated communities strung out along the coast and its inlets; I believe mail was carried, although I have yet to find anyone who can definitely confirm that; and the service brought tourists to a rugged and beautiful region. The *Northland Prince* was, in fact, the successor to generations of Canadian Pacific, Canadian National and Union Steamship vessels which had served the coast faithfully since the earliest days. (In giving its ships Prince names the Northland company was continuing a long tradition – as we have already seen in the chapter on the *Prince George*, the Canadian National ships on the coast were Princes, while the Canadian Pacific vessels were

Princesses.)

The keel of the *Northland Prince* was laid at the North Vancouver yard of the Burrard Drydock Co., Ltd. on the 14th June, 1962. Yard number 314, she was launched on the 22nd February, 1963 and delivered on the 10th June, 1963.

With her engines and passenger block aft, the *Northland Prince* had rather a stern-heavy look. This may not have been an illusion since, according to John Henderson, when she entered service she had a problem with her bow-thruster. 'When she was light-ship, it was not immersed in the sea. I believe they had to put extra ballast in her for it to work properly.' Her hull was painted dark green (later black) and her extremely low, streamlined funnel was red with a black top and a white diamond containing the letter N. Nine derricks, clustered around two sturdy bipod masts, served three holds, with some refrigerated space. A single 6-cylinder diesel engine, built by Gebroeders Stork, drove the ship at an average speed of 17.3 knots on her trials.

With 42 cabins, the ship could accommodate up to 120 passengers, including some deck passengers. Although not luxurious, the cabins were all outside and had their own facilities. There was a forward-facing dining room and there were two lounges.

In his book of sea travels, *Ocean Liner Odyssey*, Ted Scull gives a vivid description of this small vessel serving

The *St. Helena*, here seen at Cape Town, was soon given a funnel extension. *Peter Newall.*

the fishing, lumber and mining communities 'out west' and also providing tourists with a relatively cheap way of seeing the British Columbian coast. 'The ship... approached... Bella Coola, cast in the deep shadow of early evening. Several blasts from the ship's whistle, with following echoes, announced (our) arrival and soon a couple dozen cars were filing along the two mile road linking Bella Coola with its wharf. During the two-hour call, nine passengers disembarked and a considerable amount of boxed food and crated machinery was off-loaded... at Port Simpson, a remote Indian Reservation... the local kids streamed aboard to buy sweets and sodas from the vending machines... Leaving Stewart at noon we took on some very drunk prospectors and collected some more at Alice Arm. The ship originally had a public bar but because of a rough element among the passengers the company

removed it. However, alcoholic beverages could be consumed privately in the cabins, and they were.'

Tony Winstanley, who was the ship's Second Officer in 1970-1972, sheds a further light on her operation at a time when the government subsidies on which Northland depended were being called into question. 'I cannot say that my time aboard the *Northland Prince* was a happy one. There was a great deal of labour unrest and I found myself in difficult situations when, in the process of doing my job, I had to try to keep the Master happy and placate an angry crew – virtually impossible.'

It was the withdrawal of the subsidies which prompted

While the *St. Helena* was away on naval duties in the Falklands in 1982-3, Curnow Shipping used several vessels to maintain their service. One of them was the tiny *Aragonite*, photographed off Tristan da Cunha. *Father M. N. W. Edwards.*

Northland's closure of its remaining passenger services. The *Northland Prince* arrived back at Vancouver on the 30th October, 1976 after her last trip to the north. Still in the ownership of Northland Shipping (1962) Co., Ltd., she was laid up. The group then struggled on with its purely freight operations for a few more years but eventually gave up the Ghost.

The only people even remotely interested in buying the *Northland Prince* were Curnow Shipping – provided they won the St Helena contract. Eventually they did and they then clinched the deal. The ship was actually bought by United International Bank, Ltd., a subsidiary of Privatbanken, and registered in Jamestown, the capital of St Helena. Curnow set up a new company, the St Helena Shipping Co., Ltd., to manage her and to run the service.

Now called the *St. Helena*, the ship left Vancouver for the last time on the 6th November, 1977, bound for Avonmouth, where she arrived on the 5th December, carrying a cargo of lumber. She then made a trial voyage to Ascension, St Helena and Cape Town, before being taken to the Vosper Shiprepairers yard in Southampton to be fitted for her new role. To maintain the St Helena link until she was ready, small coaster-type cargo vessels were chartered and the Epirotiki Line's passenger ship *Semiramis* (2,269 gross tons, and once well-known as Elder Dempster's West African coastal liner *Calabar* and, more recently, as one of the pioneer Greek islands cruise ships) was taken up for a single voyage.

Meanwhile, the *St. Helena* was being given a surgery and hospital; a swimming pool (which was, in fact, a small circular tank placed on deck); larger fuel and water capacities; and a streamlined signal mast over the bridge. It was also intended that she should have a new and larger funnel but the idea was abandoned. (However, a year later, in September, 1979, an additional section, narrower but taller, was built onto the existing funnel.) The ship now had cabin accommodation for 76 passengers, but also carried deck passengers between St Helena and Ascension. The hull was painted khaki green, as was the 1979 extension to the funnel. All the rest of the ship above the waterline was painted white.

Having been formally re-named by Princess Margaret and taken round to Avonmouth, her new terminal port, the *St. Helena* set sail on her inaugural voyage on the 20th September, 1978 – some days later than originally intended. She arrived off St Helena on the 5th October and was greeted by large crowds and by two bands, presumably not playing simultaneously. Approval was not universal, however. One islander, used to seeing the large and imposing Union-Castle liners moored offshore, was quoted as saying, 'It seems a very odd choice. I believe it can take about 80 passengers but I don't think I'll be one of them – I'd be too scared.' Over the years, however, the little *St. Helena* – often referred to as 'the R.M.S.' because she was the last deep-sea liner still carrying Her Majesty's Mails – became a very popular ship.

Initially she called at Las Palmas but later Tenerife was substituted as her port for bunkers. The next call was Ascension where, as at St Helena, she had to anchor some way out while cargo and passengers were tendered ashore through the Atlantic swell. At St Helena, through passengers would be accommodated ashore while the ship shuttled to Ascension and back. On her first two voyages she proceeded no further than St Helena but thereafter she continued to Cape Town, thus reviving – in miniature – the old Union-Castle service. Once a year the *St. Helena* would take supplies to the even more remote island of Tristan da Cunha, 1,500 miles west of Cape Town. A ship which had been built to hug the coast of Canada was now ranging across vast expanses of open ocean.

This new career was interrupted, however, in May 1982 when she was requisitioned to act as a mother ship to two minehunters being sent south to join the British force in the Falklands War. In just 16 days at Portsmouth Naval Dockyard she was fitted with a helicopter flight deck and hangar over the stern lounge; Replenishment At Sea gear so that she could refuel and water her minehunter charges; satellite communications equipment; four Oerlikon guns plus machine guns; workshops and container loads of spare parts for the minehunters; and a myriad other things needed to fit her for her emergency role.

Finally she left Portland on the 13th June and arrived at Port Stanley on the 10th July, some time after the war had ended. By the 14th August her immediate task was completed and she and her brood left for home. However, she was then taken on time charter by the British Government and, after a refit, she returned to the Falklands for various duties both there and at South Georgia.

During their ship's absence Curnow maintained their service with several small vessels, including a British ex-coaster, the *Aragonite*, and then, more suitably, the former Blue Funnel passenger-cargo liner *Centaur*★★. The company not only chartered the 8,000-ton *Centaur* but took an option to purchase her, since it was becoming clear that the *St. Helena* was not big enough to cope with the traffic being generated. Unfortunately, the *Centaur* was suffering from mechanical problems and was badly corroded. A further factor which militated against her purchase was the design of her cargo spaces, large parts of which were intended for the carriage of livestock rather than general freight. So the option was not exercised and when the *St. Helena*'s government service ended in June, 1983 and she was handed back to Curnow in September after a refit at Falmouth, she returned to the South Atlantic route. But all concerned with the service realised that she must eventually be replaced by a larger vessel.

The first few voyages after her return were full of incident. In January, 1984 she had to shelter in Mount's Bay for three days owing to a gale; in July she was delayed at Avonmouth by a dock strike but was eventually allowed to sail (minus part of her cargo) because her service was so vital to the islanders of St Helena; in November she was disabled by a very serious engine room fire and was adrift for five days before being taken in tow for Dakar, where she remained for over a month.

---

★★For an account of the *Centaur*, see this author's *Liners & Cruise Ships: Some Notable Smaller Vessels* (Carmania Press, 1996).

By 1985 complaints were being heard about the crowded conditions in which the *St. Helena* was carrying her island passengers between St Helena and Ascension, but nevertheless she was still a well-liked ship. She continued in service until 1990, making a total of 70 round voyages (including her trips to the Falklands) and covering 840,000 miles. She was succeeded by a new *St. Helena* ★★ and after the launch of that vessel in October, 1989 the old ship was given the temporary name of *St. Helena Island*.

Not only did the service now have a larger ship with a new livery, but there was also a new home port – Cardiff – and it was there that the *St. Helena Island* ended her last voyage in October, 1990 and lay stern-to-stern with her successor. Her subsequent career was rather sad. She was quickly sold to a firm called Sea Safaris (Malta) Ltd., re-named *Avalon*, registered under the Maltese flag and placed in a new passenger-cargo service between Durban and Mombasa via Mauritius and the Comores Islands. Management of the ship remained with Curnow Shipping. Alas, the venture collapsed after a few months and the *Avalon* was laid up at Durban on the 11th June, 1991. In 1993 she was bought by Indoceanic Maritime Enterprises, Ltd. of Port Louis in Mauritius, who early in the following year re-named her *Indocéanique* and placed her in service between Mauritius and Réunion. That service did not last long either and after September, 1994 she lay idly at Port Louis until the 30th March, 1995 when she sailed for an un-named destination. She than disappears from the records until April, 1996 when she is noted as arriving at Alang to be scrapped. Work started almost immediately.

---

★★There is a chapter on the second *St Helena* in *Liners & Cruise Ships: Some Notable Smaller Vessels* (Carmania Press, 1996).

The *St. Helena* in drydock at Cape Town towards the end of her successful career on the long South Atlantic route. *Peter Newall.*

# 26

# Regina Maris

*Regina Maris | Mercator One | Frankfurt | Alexander*

Completed 1966. 5,813 gross tons. Length overall: 387 ft. 2 ins. Breadth: 53 ft. 2 ins. Draught: 16 ft. 5 ins. Twin screw. Diesel. Service speed: 20 knots. Became *Mercator One* (1976), *Frankfurt* (1979) and then *Frankfurt 1; Regina Maris* (1980); *Alexander* (1983). Converted into private yacht.

The Lübeck Line (Lübeck Linie A/G) dated back to 1924 and had a modest fleet of mainly small freighters. In 1957, however, they went into the passenger business with the *Nordland* which they had bought the previous year. At 1,800 tons, she was small and she had already seen lengthy service as the Danish *Bornholm* and as the Norwegian Hurtigruten ship *Ragnvald Jarl* belonging to the Nordenfjeldske company. However, the Germans did what they could to modernise her appearance and they improved her passenger quarters. She became, in fact, quite an important ship – the first German vessel since the War specifically intended for cruising. As such she was sufficiently successful to persuade the Lübeck Line, some years later, to order a new and larger cruise ship. They took their order to the local shipyard, the Lübecker

Flender Werke, who had already been responsible for the conversion of the *Nordland*.

The new ship was launched on the 14th December, 1965 and was called *Regina Maris*, Queen of the Sea. She was completed the following April but her initial trials may have revealed problems since she underwent a further, prolonged series the following month before entering service. Yard number 558, she was driven by a pair of MAN 10-cylinder diesel engines powerful enough to give her a service speed of a brisk 20 knots. Being purely a passenger ship, and therefore not having hatches and all the paraphernalia of cargo gear, she did not need a long bow and so the designers had been able to spread the superstructure along much of the length of the hull. It was topped off by a broad, squat funnel carrying a large smoke deflector.

For some years the *Regina Maris* was described in Lloyd's Register as a ferry and she did have space for about 40 cars in a garage towards the stern. It is doubtful if this facility was ever much used. At the time it was stated that the intention was to make it possible for cruise passengers to take their cars with them if they wished.

The *Regina Maris* was given fin stabilisers and her passenger quarters were air-conditioned. She had a

**In her early days with the Lübeck Line the *Regina Maris* gained great popularity with her German passengers.** *Laurence Dunn.*

swimming pool and a sauna and her public rooms were furnished to a high standard. She could carry up to 276 passengers, all first class and mainly in twin-berth cabins, although there were some singles. All cabins had their own toilets and wash basins and about half had either a bath or a shower. The ship was painted white except for the funnel which was black with a white band on which there were two stylised red Ls (for Lübeck Line).

On the 23rd May, 1966 the new ship left Hamburg on her first cruise – across to Leith in Scotland and then up the Norwegian coast. Subsequent cruises took her to Spain and Portugal; Norway and Iceland; and round Britain. On the 19th August, while on a Norwegian cruise, she grounded and although she did not appear to have sustained much damage she abandoned her voyage and returned to Bremerhaven for repairs. That Winter she made two long cruises: one to Rio de Janeiro and one to the Indian Ocean. In Spring, 1967 she was sailing out of Genoa. She repeated this sequence in subsequent years, except that from 1968-69 onwards the lengthy winter cruises gave way to shorter fly-cruises – passengers flew out to Tenerife to join the ship for voyages down the West African coast or round the Atlantic islands. Also every May for some years in the 'seventies there were charters to The National Trust for Scotland for their annual round-Scotland cruise.

For a few years the Lübeck Line seem to have had some success with the *Regina Maris* but by the mid-'seventies with the price of fuel oil and other costs rising alarmingly and with competition increasing, they were in difficulties. In November, 1976 they sold the ship to Canadian buyers who quickly re-named her *Mercator One*. Now registered in Bermuda in the name of Mosswood Co. Ltd. and operated by a firm called Mercator Shipping Ltd., she was to run some Caribbean cruises out of Nassau before going north for a Summer season sailing round the Canadian Maritimes. She never reached Canada. Low passenger bookings led to several of her Nassau-based cruises being cancelled and she was arrested for debt in May, 1977. She passed into the hands of the mortgagees. Eventually she was transferred to the Bahamas flag under the ownership of Mercator Enterprises Ltd. and by February, 1978 she was laid up

at Shelbourne, Nova Scotia.

Events took a more hopeful turn in October, 1979 when she was acquired for a modest Canadian $3.5million by a company associated with the adventurous German shipowner Peter Deilmann. Based in the small port of Neustadt, Deilmann had started in the cargo business in the late 'sixties and had soon moved into the passenger trade. Among his ships was a tiny vessel (only 491 gross tons) called the *Nordbrise* which he used around the Baltic and for expedition cruises to Greenland. He had much grander plans, however, and assembled a syndicate of investors to finance the construction of a new cruise ship of nearly 8,000 gross tons, to be called the *Berlin*. Within months of placing the order for that ship he also bought the former *Regina Maris* and re-named her *Frankfurt*.

Deilmann placed his purchase in the ownership of a new one-ship company, Schiffahrts ms Frankfurt GmbH, and sent her to the Nobiskrug yard in Rendsburg to be overhauled and refitted. Now all cabins had showers. Externally, the most notable change was that the funnel was now white with the Deilmann logo in red. By the time the ship was ready to enter service it had been decided that since many German passengers remembered her extremely fondly from her Lübeck Line days her name should be changed back to *Regina Maris*. She was to be marketed as a rather high-class ship.

On the 30th April, 1980 she started her new career with a Baltic cruise out of Travemunde. Others followed, and also trips up the Norwegian coast and round Britain. Deilmann had chartered her to a big German travel company for a three year series of cruises out of Singapore and in late 1980 she made her way out East via Genoa. The decision to transfer the *Regina Maris* and also the new *Berlin* to the Singapore register, thus avoiding the need to use expensive German crews (although German officers were retained), sparked off a spat with the unions. In any case, the charter was ended prematurely and by Autumn, 1981 the *Regina Maris* was back in the Mediterranean where she made a single cruise which, ironically, was marketed by an offshoot of her old owners, the Lübeck Line.

Then, in early 1982 she was chartered to a new company, Sun World Lines of St. Louis, Missouri. Marketed in the mid-Western states of America, she was to have operated Caribbean fly-cruises out of Santo Domingo. However, there was a change of plan and, instead, on the 5th June she started a programme of 7-day cruises from Montreal down the St. Lawrence and out to St.

**After being sold by the Lübeck Line the ship had a chequered career. Here she is seen in the colours of the Peter Deilmann Line**
*Clive Harvey collection.*

**She was tastefully furnished, with a great deal of wooden panelling.**
*Clive Harvey collection.*

Pierre et Miquelon. She was advertised as a luxury cruise liner – 'Interior decoration is subdued and elegant in the European style, with great use of wood panelling... Original art is hung throughout the ship. Public rooms and lounges are spacious and comfortable, evocative of the great days of the Transatlantic Liners.' But she was also intended as a gambling ship, even though gaming was not permitted in Canadian waters – hence the call at the French-owned St. Pierre et Miquelon. The Canadian authorities would have none of it, alleging that gambling was taking place as the ship sailed down the St. Lawrence. One lady passenger claimed that the police had placed agents provocateurs on board to encourage people to go to the casino so that they could obtain evidence – but that does confirm that the casino was open! At any rate, after just three cruises the ship was arrested, the purser was led off in handcuffs and the casino equipment was seized.

Eventually, the *Regina Maris* was released and later she fled to Bermuda. Still ill luck pursued her – bookings for her cruises were sparse, she was impounded and she suffered a fire. Sun World Lines gave up. For months the ship lay, unemployed, at St. George's in Bermuda.

Eventually, in May, 1983, Deilmann brought her back to Bremerhaven for repairs and then used her for a series of 7-day cruises to Norway. Later that year she was laid up at La Spezia in the hope of a further charter. However, a buyer appeared in October, 1983 and that was the end of the *Regina Maris*'s commercial career. It was a sad thing that a ship which had started so well and was so much liked by many of her passengers and crew should in the end have had so little success. Herr Deilmann has, of course, remained in the cruise business with the ultimately very successful *Berlin*, with river cruisers and even, in recent years, with a sailing ship. Now his line also has the new 20,000-ton *Deutschland*.

The buyer of the *Regina Maris* was the Greek oil and shipping tycoon John S. Latsis. Mr. Latsis is very fond of passenger ships and indeed, at one time collected them as some people collect cigarette cards. He also has very strong connections in the Arab world and in the early days he used several retired liners to act as official carriers of pilgrims making their way to the holy city of Mecca. However, he intended the former *Regina Maris* for altogether different passengers – members of the Saudi royal family were to be given the use of her as a private yacht. He named her *Alexander* after his grandson and placed her under the British flag.

It took nearly two years to plan and execute the conversion, which was undertaken by the Lloydwerft yard

**The conversion of the *Regina Maris* into the spacious and luxurious private yacht *Alexander* produced a very shapely vessel.** *Clive Harvey collection.*

**Since her conversion into a private yacht, often lent to royalty and statesmen, the ship has become a mystery vessel. Peter Knego did manage to take this clandestine photograph as she lay at Eleusis in December, 1998.**
*Peter Knego.*

in Bremerhaven. However, in August, 1985 the yacht *Alexander* was delivered to her owner. The formerly rather chunky-looking ship had been transformed into a very elegant vessel indeed. A new, sharply raked bow, streamlined masts and, above all, a much more shapely funnel had brought about this metamorphosis. There was, of course, a helicopter pad which was carried on the after end of the upper deck. Narrow sponsons now ran along the ship's sides. Little more is known of what was done to her since the work was carried out in great secrecy.

We can, however, get an inkling of what a Saudi royal yacht is like from reports which appeared in the press in 1983 when King Fahad's own yacht was being fitted out at Southampton by Vosper Thornycroft. The King was sufficiently pleased with her to make a gift of £500 to each worker and to invite them to bring their wives to see the ship. A reporter from The Times spoke to them. The visitors did not see much of the interior, except by peering through the bullet-proof windows, but, it was said that gold taps had cost £1,000 each and the light switches were also made of gold. Some table legs were also of gold, carved with lions and eagles. There were marble staircases and lapis lazuli covered the walls of the bathrooms. The visitors saw the marble swimming pool which, it was said, was a replacement for one which had been installed and then removed because it was not found pleasing. It is believed that the *Alexander* was not fitted out in quite such an extravagant style but there can be little doubt that she carries her guests in mind-boggling luxury. Just 12 passengers have the run of a 5,000-ton ship.

The *Alexander* is seen around the Mediterranean sometimes but not too much is known of her activities. Several times, however, she has figured in the press. In August, 1986 lifeboats bearing the name *Regina Maris* and carrying illegal immigrants were spotted off the coast of Newfoundland. There was some doubt as to how the occupants, who were said to be Sri Lankans, came to be there. There was no suspicion, however, that the *Alexander* was being used for illegal purposes – the lifeboats had been removed and sold during her conversion at Bremerhaven but seemingly the name *Regina Maris* had never been expunged. Then, in the early 1990s, when the marriage of Prince Charles and Princess Diana was crumbling, the *Alexander* was made available to them in order that they could attempt to sort out their problems away from the attentions of the paparazzi. On another occasion, President George Bush was a guest on board.

But the good times seemed to come to an end. Late in 1997 the Latsis family sent the *Alexander* to the Hellenic Shipyards, it was said for conversion into a cruiseship. Peter Knego saw her a year later, as yet unemployed and moored by the Latsis-controlled Petrola refinery at Eleusis. Just ahead of her was the Saudi royal yacht, *Prince Abdul-Azziz*. According to Peter, the *Alexander* was looking in a very good state, partly because 'she is coated with a special type of paint which is quite thick and gives her hull a very smooth look – almost like fiberglass. I understand that it cost a few million dollars to paint her this way.'

Whether the conversion ever took place is not clear. At any rate, in the Summer of 1999, amid much publicity, the ship was used again as a royal yacht, having been lent to Prince Charles for a Mediterranean holiday. The press worked itself into a frenzy over who would be included in the guest-list. What the future holds for the ship, however, is a mystery.

# 27

# Ocean Majesty

***Juan March / Sol Christiana / Kypros Star / Ocean Majesty***

Completed as the ferry *Juan March*, 1966. 8,983 gross tons. Length overall: 428 ft. 7 ins. Breadth: 63 ft. 1 ins. Draught: 17 ft. 9³/₄ ins. Twin screw. Diesel. Service speed: 21 knots. Became *Sol Christiana* (1985), *Kypros Star*, 6,892 gross tons (1986), *Ocean Majesty* (1989), and converted into cruise ship, 10,417 gross tons, (1990-94). Temporarily re-named *Olympic* (1994) and *Homeric* (1995), then reverted to *Ocean Majesty* (1995).

The Compañía Trasmediterránea, formed by amalgamation in 1917 and in recent years owned by the Spanish government, operates a network of services between mainland Spain, the Balearic islands, North Africa, the Atlantic islands and West Africa. In the mid-'sixties the company ordered a quartet of sleek, streamlined passenger/car ferries. The *Juan March*, named after a financier who had been much involved in Trasmediterránea, was the first to be delivered. She came from the Union Naval de Levante in Valencia, where she was yard number 93. That yard later delivered the *Las Palmas de Gran Canaria*, while the *Ciudad de Compostela* and the *Santa Cruz de Tenerife* came from a Bilbao yard. The four ships eventually became known as the 'Albatros' class.

The *Juan March* was launched on the 4th December, 1965. She was completed in July the following year and during her trials she sustained a speed of 22 knots. She had been given two 7-cylinder Burmeister & Wain diesel engines built in Barcelona by the MTM company (Maquinista Terrestre y Maritima). These drove twin controllable-pitch propellers and in addition there was a thwart-thrust unit near the bow.

Not only her upperworks were streamlined, but also the hull, with its flared bow and very rounded stern. Within that hull there was a vehicle deck, loaded through side doors and capable of holding about 100 cars or an equivalent number of commercial vehicles. In the forward section there was cargo space, some of it cooled, necessarily when the ship was carrying Canary Islands produce. Loading was by two cranes. There were also tanks for vegetable oils. Denny-Brown/AEG stabilisers were fitted.

Juan Eugenio Cañadas Bouzas, who travelled on all the 'Albatros' class ferries, remembers that 'the furnishings and decorative styles were different. Both the ships from Valencia had an austere atmosphere, with temperate colours. The two Biscayans (that is, the ships built in Bilbao) were much brighter. For me the best was the *Ciudad de Compostela* which had golden oil paintings representing the cathedral and churches of the Galician town of Compostela, and on the main staircase there was an enormous golden mural. On the *Juan March* the main lounge had a bronze bust of Juan March and murals representing the Gothic quarter of Barcelona and scenes from Majorca. But they were all elegant ships, very different from the 'plastic aesthetic' of today's Mediterranean ferries, and they were comfortable, even in bad weather conditions.'

They were built for a dual purpose – two would be used on the overnight run between Barcelona and Palma de Mallorca, one in each direction; meanwhile, the other two would maintain the express service on the much longer route between Barcelona and the Canary Islands. Passenger accommodation therefore had to be adaptable.

**Still with a large number of elderly ships, the Trasmediterránea fleet was greatly strengthened in the mid-'sixties by the advent of the four modern ferries of the 'Albatros' class, including the *Juan March*.**
*Juan Eugenio Cañadas Bouzas collection.*

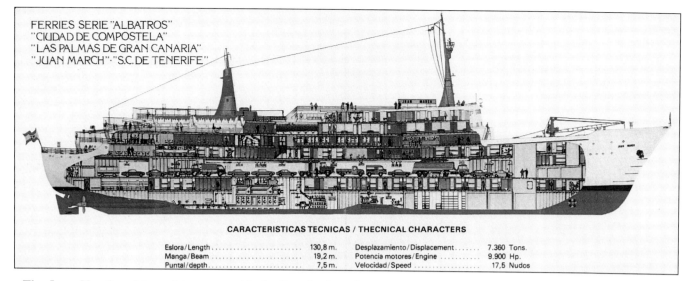

FERRIES SERIE "ALBATROS"
"CIUDAD DE COMPOSTELA"
"LAS PALMAS DE GRAN CANARIA"
"JUAN MARCH"·"S.C.DE TENERIFE"

CARACTERISTICAS TECNICAS / THECNICAL CHARACTERS

| | | | |
|---|---|---|---|
| Eslora / Length | 130,8 m. | Desplazamiento / Displacement | 7.360 Tons. |
| Manga / Beam | 19,2 m. | Potencia motores / Engine | 9.900 Hp. |
| Puntal / depth | 7,5 m. | Velocidad / Speed | 17,5 Nudos |

**The *Juan March* and her sisters were side-loading ferries of a very modern design. They were, however, eventually superseded by stern-loading vessels.** *Juan Eugenio Cañadas Bouzas collection.*

124 passengers could be carried in what was called special tourist class (often known as clase preferente or first class) consisting mainly of twin-bedded cabins with full private facilities. Ordinary tourist class could amount to 376 passengers, mainly in 4-berth cabins with wash basins but no other facilities. When, however, the ship was employed on the night run to Palma, an additional 250 passengers could be carried in the cinema-lounge where there were seats with extending head- and foot-rests.

Passenger quarters generally were of a very good standard. Brochures proclaimed 'Viaje por mar... Vacación ideal' (Sea trip... Ideal holiday) and the aim was clearly to provide something rather superior to an ordinary ferry voyage. In addition to the usual restaurants, cafeterias, lounges and bars, there was a chapel and there was also an outdoor swimming pool. On the top deck, where once the funnel might have been, was a circular observation lounge and night club – although this was later removed. Together with the twin, side-by-side, aft-mounted funnels, it gave the ship a distinctive Spanish look – very similar, in fact, to the *Cabo Izarra*, the small Ybarra Line cruise ship built about the same time. (Contemporary Scandinavian ferries had similar features but somehow they looked very different.) The *Juan March*'s hull was painted white and the slender funnels were clad in Trasmediterránea's then colours of yellow with a red band.

For some years the *Juan March* and her sisters ran very successfully, not only on the routes from Barcelona but also from Valencia. However, the introduction of newer ferries, stern-loading and with more space for cars and, in particular, trucks, caused the four sisters to be relegated to

**Like many ships from Catholic countries, the *Juan March* had a fine chapel.**
*Peter Newall collection.*

**In 1994, after her conversion into a cruise ship, the *Ocean Majesty* was chartered to Epirotiki who temporarily re-named her *Olympic*. Here she is seen at Piraeus.**
*Ambrose Greenway.*

the lesser routes to Ibiza and Minorca and other islands. Finally, in the mid-'eighties, they were put up for sale.

In 1985, the *Juan March* was bought by Sol Mediterranean Services of Limassol. This concern had been started in 1977 by a Cypriot shipping man called Takis Solomonides whose aim was to maintain a year-round Cypriot-flag ferry service in competition with marauding Greek owners who, he complained, creamed off the profitable Summer traffic and then abandoned the island in the Winter months. By the mid-'eighties, he had accumulated several second-hand ferries, including the *Juan March*'s sister *Santa Cruz de Tenerife* which he had re-named *Sol Olympia II*. Now the former *Juan March*, which he called *Sol Christiana*, joined her sister on the route from Piraeus to Heraklion, Rhodes, Limassol and Haifa. But Sol Lines were struggling and within a year the *Sol Christiana* had been sold. (The *Sol Olympia II* was destroyed by fire shortly before she too was due to be sold; and the arrest of the line's other remaining vessel marked the end of the company.)

The new owners of the former *Juan March* were another Cypriot concern, Health Shipping Co., Ltd., and in June, 1986 the ship was back in service, this time on a Piraeus – Rhodes – Limassol – Alexandria route. She was now called *Kypros Star* and operated under the trade name Opal Lines, but she seems to have suffered from a paucity of passengers during that Summer season and in 1987 and 1988 she was chartered to the Adriatica Line for their Brindisi – Patras service.

In 1989 she was transferred to the Greek flag and re-named *Ocean Majesty*. She was now registered under the ownership of Chios Breeze Marine Co., but it would seem that this was little more than a nominal change and that both as the *Kypros Star* and as the *Ocean Majesty* she has been controlled by interests connected with Mr. Michael Lambros. The plan was to convert her into a cruise ship at Perama near Piraeus, but apparently raising the necessary finance proved difficult and progress was decidedly spasmodic. A programme of cruises from Venice announced for Spring, 1991 had to be abandoned and it

was not until 1994 that the ship made her cruising debut.

The rebuilding, which it was claimed cost $36 million, involved the installation of new Wärtsilä engines and the construction of an almost completely new superstructure extending along most of the hull and built up at the stern. The former car deck is now occupied by cabins and the ship can accommodate up to 621 passengers in 273 cabins, including 8 with small balconies. Facilities include a sauna and fitness centre, disco, casino, playroom and, of course, an outdoor swimming pool. After taking a cruise in her in 1996, Jim Nurse commented that open deck space was rather limited but by 1998, when he and his wife Pat returned for another cruise, more space had been created. He says that although the *Ocean Majesty* is a high-density ship, she is very comfortable and, indeed, she does seem to have become popular with British passengers. She is also a rather attractive-looking vessel, with her new funnel structure in which the twin uptakes converge at the top.

By the time the much-interrupted conversion was completed in the Spring of 1994, the *Ocean Majesty*'s owners had given up their plans to market the ship themselves under the name Majestic Cruises, and instead they found employment for her under charter. The Epirotiki Line, having suffered the loss by fire of the *Pallas Athena* (ex-*Carla Costa*), were glad to take the *Ocean Majesty* and use her for Eastern Mediterranean cruises under the name *Olympic*. The following year, they exercised an option for a further charter and used her in the Mediterranean and in northern European waters. Several times she appeared at Dover. Having by now an *Olympic* of their own, Epirotiki re-named her *Homeric* – another name with classical connotations which was likely to remind ship-lovers of the White Star Line.

For several of her 1995 cruises Epirotiki sub-chartered the ship to the British holiday firm Page & Moy and each year since then Page & Moy have chartered her direct from her owners for a season of Summer cruises, now under her own name of *Ocean Majesty*. There have been other charters, to Dutch, Belgian and Italian firms – although

the latter had to curtail a programme of Red Sea cruises in the Winter of 1995 owing to poor bookings. In 1997 the *Ocean Majesty* was chartered by Orient Line for some cruises in Greek and Turkish waters. (The previous year, Orient's own *Marco Polo* had met fierce opposition from the Greek seamen's union when she had tried to operate a similar programme. Clearly this time Orient Line were taking no chances and decided to use a Greek-flag vessel.) The *Ocean Majesty* is also being tried as a long-distance cruise ship. She has visited the Caribbean and for 1999-2000 she has been chartered by Marine Expeditions for an ambitious 'Millennium Cruise'. It is claimed that this will be the first time a cruise has called at all seven continents, including Antarctica.

The *Ocean Majesty* is not the only one of the 'Albatros' class quartet to be turned into a cruise-ship. The former *Las Palmas de Gran Canaria*, much converted, now operates under the rather racy name of *Don Juan* (latterly *D. Juan*), mainly carrying Spanish passengers.

But to revert to the *Ocean Majesty* herself – she shews signs of becoming one of those ships, like *Black Prince* or *Funchal*, which may not be outstanding or glamorous, but which attract a loyal band of middle-aged, middle class, middle brow followers who find the atmosphere on board extremely congenial.

**The *Ocean Majesty* is a high-density ship, but a very comfortable one.**
*Jim Nurse.*

# 28

# Calypso

*Canguro Verde | Durr | Ionian Harmony | Sun Fiesta | Calypso*

Completed 1967 as the ferry *Canguro Verde*. 5,223 gross tons. Length overall: 414 ft. 6 ins. Breadth: 63 ft. 2 ins. Draught: 16 ft. 10 ins. Twin screw. Diesel. Service speed: 18½ knots. Became *Durr* (1981); *Ionian Harmony* (1989); *Sun Fiesta* (1990). Rebuilt as cruise ship *Regent Jewel*, 1993, 11,162 gross tons. Became *Calypso* (1994).

In September, 1998 I saw the *Norway* and the *Splendour Of The Seas*★★ at Lisbon – two of the World's biggest passenger ships, yet among the most elegant. Five days later, back in Greenwich, I saw the *Calypso* – tiny in comparison with those behemoths, yet infinitely more ungainly. Ironically, before her conversion into a cruise ship she had been a very shapely ferry, one of a group of Italian vessels which were not only attractive to the eye but also very notable. She had been built for a new line set up to compete with the established, state-owned Tirrenia company on the routes linking Sardinia with the mainland of Italy and, in particular, to provide roll-on, roll-off facilities for cars and for larger vehicles.

The new company was called Traghetti Sardi (i.e.: Sardinia Ferries) and orders for three vessels were placed with the Navalmeccanica shipyard at Castellammare di Stabia (which in 1967 came under the aegis of the giant new state-owned combine Italcantieri). The design of the new ships was an improved version of that for two other ferries which the yard had built for a sister company of Traghetti Sardi which ran a similar service between Naples and Palermo. Both groups were given Kangaroo names – *Canguro Azzurro* (Blue Kangaroo) and *Canguro Rosso* (Red Kangaroo) for the Sicilian ships and *Canguro Verde* (Green Kangaroo), *Canguro Bianco* (White Kangaroo) and *Canguro Bruno* (Brown Kangaroo) for the Sardinians. Naturally, they were known as the Canguro Line and the ships had the image of the animal painted on their hulls. A further service, between Genoa and Barcelona, was run in conjunction with the Spanish company Ybarra and when the Spaniards introduced

a new ferry of their own onto the route she was called *Canguro Cabo San Sebastian*, thus rather ponderously combining the Kangaroo nomenclature with Ybarra's traditional Cabo (i.e.: Cape) naming system. It was all a clever marketing ploy designed to highlight the way in which the new ships could carry motor vehicles in vast garages within their hulls, rather like the way the marsupial mum carries her baby in her pouch. It was not an exact analogy, though, since the Sardinian ships were stern-loaders whereas the kangaroo is a front-loader.

As we have already noted, the *Canguro Verde* and her sisters were good-looking ships. Their domed, finned and heavily ventilated funnels, rather stylish and very Italian, were similar to those on the big Lloyd Triestino liners *Galileo Galilei* and *Guglielmo Marconi* and on the later 'Poeti' class of ferries – unsurprisingly since they were all the result of experimental work done at Turin Polytechnic under Professor Mortarino.

The car deck could accommodate 104 cars or 41 lorry trailers. Passenger capacity was 700, 334 in cabins and 366 in reclining seats. There was partial air-conditioning. Two 7-cylinder FIAT Grandi Motori diesel engines drove twin controllable-pitch propellers and there were also thwart-thrust propellers both fore and aft. The ship was fitted with fin stabilisers.

The *Canguro Verde* was the first of the Sardinian sisters. She was launched on the 23rd April, 1967 and, registered

---

★★Why, one wonders, was a ship intended for the American market given the English spelling, *Splendour*, rather than the American *Splendor*?

The *Canguro Verde*, ready for launching at Castellammare, near Naples, on the 23rd April, 1967.
*Admeto Verde collection.*

The *Canguro Verde* at her berth at Porto Torres in Sardinia in August, 1970.
*D. Audibert photograph, Ambrose Greenway collection.*

at Cagliari, she was handed over to her owners in the September.

The three ships jointly ran services between Genoa and Cagliari, Genoa and Porto Torres and Genoa and Barcelona. Capable of more than 21 knots and well able to cater for the burgeoning motor traffic, they were an immediate success. There were two results – Traghetti Sardi and its sister company both built an additional ferry (similar to the existing Kangaroos, but with diesel-electric propulsion) plus some ro-ros to deal with the growing lorry traffic; and the state company Tirrenia, which had been badly affected by the new competition, was spurred into ordering a new class of ferries which could match the Kangaroos in speed and in vehicle capacity. They were called 'Poeti', since they were named after writers.

The advent of the 'Poeti' curtailed the success of the Kangaroos. In 1974 Traghetti Sardi and its sister company merged, forming Società Linee Canguro S.p.A. Some of the ships were chartered (and in some cases eventually sold) to Tirrenia and the Sicilian service was abandoned. *Canguro Verde* and *Canguro Bianco*, however, remained on the Genoa – Port Torres and Genoa – Cagliari routes, for a time under charter to Tirrenia.

In late 1981, *Canguro Verde* was sold to Fayez Trading

'Will there be anything more, sir?' A carefully posed scene from a Canguro Line brochure. *Peter Newall collection.*

& Shipping of Jeddah, who placed her under the Saudi flag and re-named her *Durr*. The following year, the sale of the *Canguro Bruno* (also to Fayez, who called her *Yum*) marked the end of the Canguro Line. The two ships were placed in Red Sea service, mainly from Suez or Aqaba to Jeddah, but with occasional voyages from Port Sudan and elsewhere. They were no doubt particularly busy during the annual pilgrim season. They were not greatly altered, although the *Durr*'s passenger capacity was now listed as 358 berths and no less than 1,160 deck passengers.

The *Durr* started her Red Sea career in December, 1981 and presumably performed satisfactorily since the Fayez company bought her sister a year later. However, in November, 1982 the *Durr* was immobilised when a seawater pipe burst, and the resultant flooding caused expensive damage to electric motors and generators. The ship was towed to Malta for repairs and remained there until February, 1983. In August, 1983 she had a minor collision with another Red Sea ferry, the *Al-Qamar Al-Saudi II*, but otherwise led a fairly uneventful life. Competitors

The former *Canguro Verde* saw brief service as the Red Sea ferry *Durr*. *Antonio Scrimali.*

included the ships of the Vlasov-controlled Saudi Maritime Transport Company.

The *Durr* and the *Yum* remained with Fayez until 1989, when they were sold to Strintzis Lines, the Greek ferry operators. The *Durr* left the Red Sea in February and was quickly re-named *Ionian Harmony* and placed on the Maltese register. *Yum*, on the other hand, joined the Greek register, at first as the *Ionian Fantasy* and later as the *Ionian Sea*.

Unlike her sister, the *Ionian Harmony* (ex-*Durr*) did not remain long with Strintzis. After two seasons on the Ancona – Patras route, often via Yugoslav ports, she was sold in October, 1990 for use by the Danish Cruise Line, a new concern trying to establish a short-cruise service out of San Juan to St. Thomas in the Virgin Islands. The new company was a joint venture between a Danish ferry-operator, Nordisk Faergefart, and SeaEscape Cruises, well-known for their short trips out of Florida ports. The *Ionian Harmony* was called *Sun Fiesta*, registered in the Bahamas and owned by Ferry Charter St. Thomas Ltd. Probably because of the financial problems of SeaEscape, she never entered service, but remained, partially converted, at a shipyard in Mobile. Eventually she was seized by the U.S. Admiralty Marshal and several attempts were made to sell her by auction. In the end, in 1992, she was bought by interests connected with Anthony Lelakis, a then very prominent Greek shipowner.

Then called the *Regent Jewel*, the former ferry was converted into a cruise ship at Chalkis in Greece in 1993-94. *Antonio Scrimali.*

Mr. Lelakis, who was best known for his Regency Cruise Line, was in the habit of buying elderly passenger vessels cheaply and spending quite heavily on fitting them for the less expensive end of the cruise market. He had *Sun Fiesta* towed to Greece, to the Avlis shipyard at Chalkis (leased by his group). There ensued a complete remodelling of the ship, including the addition of two extra decks which were no doubt very worthwhile commercially but were unfortunate from an aesthetic point of view. They were topped by a blockish funnel crowned by

several extension pipes. The angular ferry stern was retained, although now closed up. The overall result was a chunky, piled-up ship, recognisably from the same stable as the *Regent Rainbow* which the same yard had just created out of old Grace Line *Santa Rosa*. But if the transformation of the former *Canguro Verde* was not entirely happy, it was as nothing compared with the disaster inflicted on her old rivals, the 'Poeti', when Tirrenia had them rebuilt, as the accompanying photographs shew.

The ex-*Canguro Verde* was re-engined during her re-construction, being given two Wärtsilä V-12 units. Fitted out to carry 593 passengers in 243 rather small cabins, she acquired most of the usual cruise ship facilities – two deck-high lounge, bars, casino, gymnasium, swimming pool. She was decorated in the current fashion, with shiny metal ceilings. She is said to be a rather pleasant ship. The original

The *Canguro Verde*'s old rivals, the 'Poeti' ferries of the Tirrenia Line, suffered an even more drastic (and hideous) reconstruction. *Ambrose Greenway; Laurence Dunn collection; and Ambrose Greenway.*

intention was that she should be called *Regent Moon* but, instead, she was registered in the Bahamas as the *Regent Jewel* in the ownership of a Lelakis company, Jewel Cruises, Inc., sometimes spelled Jule. It was proposed that she should enter service in Spring, 1994 with a series of week-long cruises out of Piraeus and Istanbul. However, completion was delayed and when she finally emerged, in the October, she had undergone a name change to *Calypso* and had been chartered to Transocean Cruises, whose logo she wore on her funnel. Carrying mainly German passengers, she embarked on a programme of Far Eastern cruises out of Singapore, followed by some Northern European cruises. The first few months were not without incident – in July, 1995 she grounded off the coast of Norway and had to retreat to a dry dock in Bremerhaven. In August she limped back to Bremerhaven with engine trouble.

However, when in October, 1995 the Lelakis bubble burst, she was the only one of the six Regency Cruise Line ships not arrested. Having acquired at least ten passenger vessels in as many years, the Lelakis group had been overwhelmed by debt. Unlike most of her fleetmates, which passed into the ownership of the banks or other financial houses to which they had been mortgaged, the *Calypso* did not immediately change hands. As long as the five-year charter to Transocean continued to produce a steady flow of income, the ship remained with her owners.

**With bright, metallic, contemporary décor, the *Calypso*, as she had now become, achieved some popularity in the German cruise market.** *Marc Tragbar.*

When, however, the charter expired in Autumn, 1998 and was not renewed, she was quickly arrested and became the property of the National Bank of Greece. An attempt to sell her by auction in April, 1999 was not successful and at the time of writing the *Calypso* lies, idle, near Piraeus, awaiting the next phase of her already unusually varied career.

**Arrested for debt, the *Calypso* lies near Piraeus in December, 1998. The built-up, blockish superstructure she acquired during her reconstruction does little for her appearance.** *Peter Knego.*

# 29

# Lindblad Explorer

***Lindblad Explorer / Society Explorer / Explorer***
Completed as *Lindblad Explorer*, 1969. 2,481 gross tons. Length overall: 239 ft. 1 ins. Breadth: 46 ft. 0 ins. Draught: 13 ft. 9¼ ins. Single screw. Diesel. Service speed: 15 knots. Became *Society Explorer* (1985). Became *Explorer* (1992).

It would not be quite true to say that expedition cruising began in 1969. As early as 1879 a small Norwegian steamer made a cruise to Spitzbergen and later, as cruising developed, some quite remote places became familiar destinations for the more enquiring kind of passenger. In the past forty years, the mushroom growth of tourism, brought about by increasing affluence and the advent of the jet aeroplane, has meant that once far-flung and exciting places have become almost commonplace destinations. (Just how far tourism has come was brought home to me a few years ago on a cruise I took on the comfortable *Black Prince* in order to see the wonders of Spitzbergen. There we were, nearing 80°N, and still passengers were swimming in the ship's heated outdoor pool!)

But as the extraordinary has steadily become more ordinary, there are still people who crave for the sense of adventure which those early cruisers to Spitzbergen must have felt in 1879. And as interest has grown in the environment and what we are doing to it, more people have formed the desire to see Antarctica and the few other remaining 'last frontiers' for themselves. It is obviously a

limited market, but it is a growing one. I have seen it stated that over 6,000 people visited Antarctica in 1996. In comparison with the count for, say, the Bahamas, that is not very many but it is, in fact, a very large number. Perhaps the first entrepreneur to sniff the wind was Lars-Eric Lindblad in the 1960s. The career of the *Lindblad Explorer*, however – the first ship specifically dedicated to his cruises – illustrates the risks, both physical and financial, which expedition cruising involves.

The contract for her building went to a small Finnish yard, Nystads Varv. of Nystad, otherwise Uuisikaupunki, in the Gulf of Bothnia where there was plenty of experience of dealing with ships which operated in extreme ice conditions. The owners of the new vessel were a concern called K/S A/S Explorer & Co. managed by Lars Usterud-Svendsen of Oslo and she flew the Norwegian flag. She was launched on the 18th June, 1969 and was ready to enter service by December that year, under charter to Lindblad Travel, Inc.

Although topped by a modern, streamlined radar and signal mast and a raked funnel, the little *Lindblad Explorer* looked a very solid, purposeful ship. The hull, double-skinned and with the highest ice classification, was painted orange red – a colour much used among Arctic and Antarctic vessels since in the event of trouble it makes them conspicuous and easier to find. Two MaK 8-cylinder diesel engines were geared to a single controllable-pitch propeller. There was a bow thruster and at the stern there was an ice knife, a device intended to

**One of the pioneers of modern expedition cruising, the *Linblad Explorer* was built with a specially ice-strengthened hull.** *Luis Miguel Correia.*

**It is the ship's cruises in polar regions, particularly in the Antarctic, which have made her famous.**
*Mark Goldberg collection.*

protect the rudder from damage. A conspicuous feature was the enclosed crow's nest on the mast – although this was eventually removed. Intended to operate in very remote areas, the *Lindblad Explorer* had to be a particularly self-sufficient vessel. She also had to pollute the pristine environment through which she would be sailing as little as possible. In recent years the expedition cruise lines have observed a voluntary code of 'good practice' in this respect.

Life for the *Lindblad Explorer*'s 120 passengers** was intended to be comfortable and relatively informal. They were accommodated in smallish double cabins, all of them outside so that the occupants could observe the passing scene, and all of them with private facilities. The public rooms, although not luxurious, were said to be well-decorated and included a substantial reference library. Each cruise had naturalists, scientists or explorers on board to lecture and to guide. The aim was to interest and instruct while carrying the passengers in comfortable surroundings. Other vessels which have since entered this market have tended to be somewhat more luxurious.

The brand new *Lindblad Explorer* left Nystad in mid-December, 1969, calling first at Southampton before starting the long trek southwards to Buenos Aires which she reached on the 11th January, having been delayed by generator problems and a galley fire. She then made two sorties to Antarctica, one from Port Stanley in the Falklands and one from Punta Arenas. This was the first of the many Southern Hemisphere Summer seasons she has spent in that area. Then, between March and December, 1970 she was occupied with Indian Ocean cruises out of Mombasa, a programme she repeated the following year, having in the meantime been based in Australian ports for her 1971 Antarctic season. In later years, she has cruised up the Amazon, not just to Manaos but as far as Iquitos in Peru, and she has visited the South Pacific, the Indonesian islands, the Alaskan coast and China. There have also been cruises in less exotic areas, but always calling at out-of-the-way ports. However, it has been her Arctic and Antarctic voyages which have made her famous.

Almost inevitably, such adventurous voyaging has produced mishaps, at least one of which was critically serious. On the 11th February, 1972, she ran aground, while cruising off King George Island in the South Shetland Archipelago in the Antarctic with a full complement of passengers. She was seriously holed, the engine room was flooded, the rudder was damaged and the propeller shaft was forced out of alignment. Conditions were bad, with snow and winds of up to 90 kph. Two Chilean naval vessels, two Argentine Navy ships, *H.M.S. Endurance*, an American and a Russian ship all hurried towards her. The Chileans made four unsuccessful attempts to refloat her and one of them, the *Piloto Pardo*, eventually took her passengers and most of her crew to Punta Arenas. Meanwhile, the salvage tug *Arctic* was making her way from Cape Town and arrived on the scene or the 23rd February. The leaks were temporarily patched and on her second attempt the *Arctic* succeeded in refloating the ship. She towed her slowly to Buenos Aires, where they arrived on the 10th March. There the *Lindblad Explorer* was dry-docked before being towed by the tug *Baltic* all the way to Kristiansund S. in Norway for permanent repairs.

Meanwhile, her owners had sold her in her still damaged state, to the United Cruising Co., Ltd. of Bermuda (an offshoot of the Swedish American Line, which in turn was controlled by the Broström group of Gothenberg) together with a new company called Lindblad Explorer S.A. Paul Pålsson remembers that when Lars-Eric Lindblad was asked whether the grounding would affect bookings for future cruises, he replied that it would make the ship more popular than ever! Mr. Pålsson also comments 'The very experienced Swedish officers and crew did a lot to popularise her cruises. A job on board the *Lindblad Explorer* was much sought after. It was rather odd for a ship now registered

---

**In fact, she usually carries no more than 95 passengers, with the other cabins being occupied by tour leaders, lecturers, etc.

under the Panamanian flag to have an expensive, mainly Swedish crew.'

On Christmas Day, 1979 the *Lindblad Explorer* was aground in the Antarctic again, this time on Wiencke Island, not too far from the scene of her previous ordeal. Again her engine room was flooded and again the *Piloto Pardo* took off her passengers and most of her crew. This time, after two days the *Lindblad Explorer* was pulled free by a Russian tug, the *Uragan*. After makeshift repairs in a sheltered bay on King George Island, she was towed to a dockyard at Talcahuano. As on the previous occasion, a major mishap was followed by a change of ownership – Broström sold the ship to The China Navigation Company, the shipping arm of John Swire & Sons, Ltd.** The new arrangement did not last long, for in July, 1982 China Navigation bowed out and the ship was sold to the Salén group of Sweden. She now flew the Swedish flag. The charter to Lindblad Travel ceased and marketing was now handled by Salén Lindblad Cruising, a quite separate firm despite the similarity of name.

In 1984, the *Lindblad Explorer* made a historic voyage. On the 20th August she sailed from St. John's, Newfoundland in an attempt on the North West Passage, the hazardous sea route through the polar waters north of Canada. When she arrived at Point Barrow, Alaska on the 14th September she became, it was said, the first passenger ship ever to make the passage and, indeed only the 34th vessel of any kind to do so. 98 passengers had paid up to $20,000 each for the 41-day voyage which ended at Yokohama, a distance of 4,790 miles. It is said that the ship was fully booked within days of the expedition being announced and that on reaching Point Barrow the crew celebrated by shaving off the beards they had been growing since the voyage commenced. Two months later the ship was at the other end of the globe, sailing in Antarctic waters. Just how hazardous the polar seas can be is shewn by the fact that in August, 1988 she was trapped in pack ice in the Beaufort Sea. Fortunately, she managed to free herself.

By then, she had changed hands on a further two occasions. Soon after completing her epic 1984 voyage through the North West Passage, she was sold to a joint venture between Society Expeditions and the Heritage Hotel group. Within a few months, however, she was bought by Vienna International Shipping Corporation and registered in Liberia. The new company was associated with Discoverer Reederei of Bremen, the owners of the rival expedition ship, *World Discoverer*. The original intention was that the *Lindblad Explorer* should be renamed *World Explorer*, but in September, 1985 she emerged from a major four-month refit at Singapore with the name *Society Explorer* and registered in the Bahamas. She had been chartered back to Society Expeditions. She now had a more angular funnel adorned by the Discoverer badge – a globe containing the letter D. Her accommodation now included two suites.

In August, 1986 the *Society Explorer* made several cruises which included stays at Vancouver for passengers to visit Expo '86 and then continued up the inside passage along the coast of British Columbia. In January, 1989 the ship was involved in another Antarctic incident, but this time as a rescuer not a victim. She and the *Illiria* took on board 81 passengers from the Argentine Navy supply and tourist ship *Bahia Paraiso* which sank in the the Bismarck Strait.

But Discoverer Reederei and Society Expeditions were encountering financial difficulties. In March, 1991 the *Society Explorer* was seized by creditors while in a shipyard at Santiago and remained under arrest for several months. Discoverer, meanwhile, refused delivery of the ambitious new *Society Adventurer* which they had ordered from a Finnish yard. (She eventually became Hapag-Lloyd's *Hanseatic*.) In January, 1992 Society Expeditions filed for Chapter 11 protection from their creditors and in March, at the end of the Antarctic season, withdrew their two vessels. The *World Discoverer* was chartered to the Clipper Cruise Line and the *Society Explorer* was sold to another firm specialising in exotic and cultural holidays, Abercrombie & Kent.

Now called the *Explorer* and flying the Liberian flag, this important little ship continues to operate much as she has done throughout her now quite long career. In June, 1995 she visited a number of British and Irish ports while making two round-Britain cruises, but it is for her polar voyages that she is best known.

---

**Paul Pålsson, who was by then Chief Executive of Broström, says however, that it was rising costs as much as the grounding which prompted the decision to sell to China Navigation who had been expressing interest for some time.

The *Explorer*, as she is now known, emerged from a major refit in 1985 with a rebuilt funnel and various other modifications. Note the rubber zodiacs aft of the funnel.
*Luís Miguel Correia.*

# 30

# Rangatira

### *Rangatira / Queen M / Carlo R.*

Completed, 1972. 9,387 gross tons. Length overall: 500 ft. 9 ins. Breadth: 72 ft. 5 ins. Draught: 17 ft. 4 ins. Twin screw. Turbo-electric. Service speed: 21 knots. Became *Queen M* (1986), *Carlo R.* (1990).

The *Rangatira* has not been a lucky ship. She was born under tragic circumstances and her owners must often have felt that she was a white elephant, a burden. Even so, she has had her times of usefulness – and profit. She was built for the Union Steam Ship Company of New Zealand's fast service between Wellington on the North Island and Lyttelton on the South Island. New Zealand may be a remote country, but Union Steam Ship, founded in 1875, has been a world-famous company with services stretching far beyond the local coasts. It became a subsidiary of the P & O Group of London in 1917. In 1965 the company introduced drive-on / drive-off facilities on the Wellington – Lyttelton route, and the following year added a spectacular new ferry to the service, the *Wahine*. In April, 1968 the *Wahine* was blown onto a reef while attempting to enter Wellington harbour in a terrific gale. She sank and 51 lives were lost. It was to replace this tragic ship that the *Rangatira* was built.

The contract went to Swan Hunter Shipbuilders, Ltd. for the vessel to be constructed at their Walker yard on the Tyne. In order to qualify for financial assistance from the British government she was to be owned and registered in Britain by a concern called the Union Steam Ship Company (U.K.) Ltd. With her very streamlined profile, the *Rangatira* was an obvious near-relative of the lost *Wahine*, but various recommendations made at the Court of Inquiry into the disaster were heeded. In particular, the drainage system on the vehicle decks was improved in order to reduce what is known as the free surface effect (the way in which a relatively small amount of water admitted to the vast, undivided spaces of a car deck can wash around with a dangerously de-stabilising result).

The Union company had for many years been enthusiasts for the turbo-electric propulsion system, at any rate for the ships they ordered for the Wellington – Lyttelton service. At both ends of the route it was necessary to dock stern-first and the ability of turbo electric vessels to manoeuvre rapidly in reverse was obviously useful. Also, their quietness and smooth-running was ideal for an overnight service. The entire

**Bearing a marked similarity to her lost predecessor, the *Wahine*, the *Rangatira* had a sleek, modern appearance.**
*Laurence Dunn collection.*

The *Rangatira* making her maiden arrival at Wellington on the 18th March, 1972. She entered Union Steamship's ferry service between the north and south islands of New Zealand when it was already in decline. *Victor Young and Len Sawyer.*

propulsion system for the *Rangatira* – steam turbines, generators, electric motors – was built by Associated Electrical Industries, part of the GEC group. To aid manoeuvrability, the ship was fitted with twin rudders and with two sets of bow-thrusters. Like the Isle of Man Steam Packet Company, another concern not afraid to be unorthodox if there seemed good reason, the Union company specified steam-powered thrusters rather than the usual electric ones. The ship was fitted with Denny-Brown AEG stabilisers.

The Wellington – Lyttelton service had been mainly an overnight run. Accordingly, the *Rangatira* had limited open deck space and was fitted with large numbers of small cabins. Deep in the hull there were also several multi-berth rooms intended for parties of school children. In all, the ship had berths for 768 passengers. She would also have to make some daytime sailings, however, and so she was given additional space for 'deck passengers'. The public rooms consisted of a self-service cafeteria, two grill rooms, a smoke room and a lounge. A cinema was added later. When the ship arrived in New Zealand there was favourable comment on the furnishing of these public rooms, particularly the lounge looking out over the stern of the ship. The vehicle decks could carry up to 200 cars or an equivalent number of cars, commercial vehicles and pallets of freight. Access was through a stern door, the company preferring not to have a bow door in view of the fierce seas the ship was likely to encounter on this route. Very unusually for a passenger ferry, the *Rangatira* was given tanks for the carriage of small cargoes of lubricating oil.

The *Rangatira* was launched on the 23rd June, 1971 – later than planned. She ran her sea trials in December but

was still not complete owing to a strike of insulation workers. In the end the owners accepted the ship in her unfinished state and on the 14th January, 1972 sailed her out of the Tyne and took her to Southampton where, at Berth 30, she was completed. She reached Wellington (via the Panama Canal) on the 18th March and proceeded to damage herself while attempting a trial docking. Finally, on the 28th March, she entered service.

Meanwhile, there had been two developments. P & O had sold their shares in Union Steam Ship to Australian and New Zealand interests. And it had become clear that the Wellington – Lyttelton route was in serious decline. Partly, perhaps, because of the *Wahine* disaster passengers with cars were tending to favour the shorter Wellington – Picton service operated by New Zealand Railways; and passengers travelling without cars were increasingly taking to the plane when crossing from one island to the other. By the time the *Rangatira* was ready the company had abandoned its plan to resume the old nightly service with one ship sailing in each direction. Accordingly the *Maori*, which had been carrying on the service single-handedly, was laid up.

The *Rangatira*, which had cost £4.8 million, wore the traditional Union Steam Ship livery of dark green hull and red funnel with a black top and two thin black bands. Unhappily, her ill-luck persisted and she was plagued by problems with her turbines. After just six months she had to be taken out of service for repairs and the *Maori* was brought temporarily out of reserve until the *Rangatira* returned in October, 1972. The Wellington – Lyttelton route was losing money heavily. Eventually, a government subsidy was forthcoming but this was not renewed in 1976 and so the service was closed, the *Rangatira* making her

The *Rangatira* has had considerably more success as an accommodation ship than as a ferry. Here she is seen during her stint as a floating barracks at Port Stanley in the Falklands.
*Captain William Houghton-Boreham.*

final arrival at Wellington on the 15th September after just 4½ years on the route.

She did not linger there. Her owners had decided to bring her back to England and offer her for sale. She left Wellington on the 17th September and exactly a month later arrived at Falmouth where she was laid up. Perhaps because she was known to be thirsty and was suspected of being unreliable, she did not attract a buyer. She did, however, find employment. From March, 1977 to May, 1978 she was chartered as an accommodation ship at the Howard-Dorris oil-rig construction site in Loch Kishorn. After that, she was laid up in Glasgow but soon gained another charter. British Petroleum were developing a terminal for their North Sea oil and gas fields at Sullom Voe in the Shetlands. They needed an accommodation ship to house construction workers and so they chartered the *Rangatira* and spent £700,000 on refitting her. She remained at Sullom Voe, latterly in company with the *Stena Baltica*, from September, 1978 to July, 1981. The Union Steam Ship Company (U.K.)'s accounts shew that during her stays at Loch Kishorn and Sullom Voe the *Rangatira* was very profitable and that the company had no difficulty in repaying large instalments of the government loan with which she had been built. Unfortunately the North Sea oil boom subsided and British Petroleum cancelled the final phase of the Sullom Voe project.

The *Rangatira* arrived back at Falmouth on the 5th July, 1981 and was laid up. At one time there was hope of employment as an accommodation ship off the coast of Mexico; and she was inspected by South African interests who considered converting her into a cruise ship. Then, in April, 1982 the Argentine invaded the Falklands and Britain went to war. The battlefield was 8,000 miles away and large numbers of merchant ships became 'stuft' (ships taken up from trade) in order to transport troops, weapons and supplies to the battle zone. Some 50 vessels were snatched from their civilian employment, including some famous ships which performed heroic deeds – the *QE2*, the *Canberra*, the *Uganda*, the *Norland* and others. The owners of the unemployed *Rangatira* must have hoped that she, too, would be taken up, but at first she was not thought suitable. However, in mid-May – with more troops needing to be sent and, perhaps, with thought already being taken as to how to maintain a garrison in the Falklands once the war had been won – the call came. On the 23rd May the *Rangatira* was taken to the Plymouth Naval Dockyard which had already performed wonders of speedy conversion of several merchant ships. She remained there until the 14th June. The stern lounge was removed and replaced by a helicopter pad; watertight bulkheads were built across the vehicle deck – importantly,

Rush hour in the Falklands. EMF (embarked military forces) are ferried back to their floating home, the accommodation ship *Rangatira*.
*Captain William Houghton-Boreham.*

since she was going to war and might sustain damage; Replenishment At Sea equipment was installed so that she could be refuelled while en route; more bunks were squeezed into many of the cabins, increasing the capacity to nearly 1,400; mess-decks, refrigerated stores, extra fresh-water plant, more generators and all the other necessary paraphernalia were installed – all in not much more than three weeks. She was to be managed by Blue Star Ship Management.

On the 19th June the ship left Southampton fully laden with service personnel, mainly Royal Engineers. The war was already over – it had ended on the 14th – but there was plenty of use for the *Rangatira* after she arrived at Port Stanley on the 11th July. Once again in the role of an accommodation ship, she remained at anchor until September, 1983, helping to house and feed the garrison which Britain now maintained on the Falklands. She was, in fact, the last of the STUFT ships to return home, and then only because she had been replaced by more permanent accommodation barges – two of which were owned by the Bibby Line.

Captain Bill Houghton-Boreham who served on the *Rangatira* during this period remembers that 'the uncomplimentary nickname given to the ship by many of her temporary lodgers was 'Rangatraz'. It was not unusual for the vessel to accommodate up to 1,000 souls on any particular night. We had a 'rush hour' in the morning and late afternoon as the 'embarked military forces' (EMF) made their way to and from their daily tasks. The flight deck was built to withstand landings by Sea King helicopters but the occasional touchdown by a Chinook would usually result in sections of the deckhead panelling of the EMF mess dropping off! Once every six weeks or so, we would leave our moorings in Stanley Harbour to refuel from the tanker *Scottish Eagle* in Berkley Sound. During the time on passage the ship's naval party exercised the anti-aircraft armament by trying to hit a parachute flare launched from the bridge. On one occasion the target, launched to windward by error, descended, unmolested by 'friendly fire', and lodged itself in a coiled-up boat embarkation ladder. The *Rangatira* might have become the only ship on record ever to be destroyed by a target! Fortunately, the blaze was extinguished by a passing seaman. The ship's engineers ran a cottage industry producing brass ashtrays from spent artillery shells, inlaid with Falklands coins (one of which rests on our lounge coffee table today).'

The *Rangatira* arrived back at

Plymouth on the 18th October, 1983. Four days later she entered the Harland & Wolff shipyard at Belfast to be restored to her pre-Falklands condition. This took over five months. Finally, on the 30th March, 1984 and once again in the hands of her owners, she was laid up at Falmouth. She remained idle for over $2^{1}/_{2}$ years. There was talk that she might be converted into a cruise ship but nothing came of it. Eventually, in November, 1986, she was sold to Searoyal, a Cypriot-registered company within the Marlines group, Greek ferry operators owned by the Marangopoulos family. Named *Queen M*, she was much less altered than most Greek ferry purchases, the main addition being a slight extension of one deck of superstructure at the stern. She was placed in service on possibly the busiest of the routes across the Adriatic – that between Ancona, Igoumenitsa and Patras.

The *Queen M* remained with Marlines for three seasons. It was announced that in 1990 she would be used on the longer route between Ancona, Patras and Turkish ports but, instead, she was sold to the Rodriquez group of Messina in Sicily. They were best-known as builders of large hydrofoils but they had recently gone into the ferry-operating business through a subsidiary called Alimar. They called their new purchase the *Carlo R.* and registered her under the Maltese flag. In the Summers of 1990, 1991 and 1992 they chartered her to Cotunav, the Tunisian state shipping company who used her in their services between Tunis and Genoa and Tunis and Marseilles. When the charter was not renewed for 1993, Alimar tried operating her themselves between Italian ports and Tunis. This was said to have been very successful but the following season she was chartered to a new Greek firm called Horizon Sea Lines for a service between Ancona and Cesme in Turkey. In Summer, 1995 she was to have run for Egnatia Line in a similar service but by now the Rodriquez group was in financial difficulties and Egnatia Line did not proceed with the charter. The *Carlo R.* made a few voyages from Bari to Patras, but was then laid up at Naples and has remained there ever since, for much of the time under arrest. As so often in the past the ship faces an uncertain future.

**Probably the last steam-powered ferry in the Mediterranean, the *Carlo R* lies, laid up and under arrest, at Naples in October, 1997.** *Mike Lennon.*

# 31

# Aquarius

### Aquarius / Adriana

Completed,1972 as *Aquarius*. 4,591 gross tons. Length overall: 340 ft. 3 ins. Breadth: 45 ft. 11 ins. Draught: 14 ft. 1¼ . ins. Twin screw. Diesel. Service speed: 19½ knots. Became *Adriana* (1987).

In October, 1997 the ship-repairing quarter of the port of Genoa was positively crammed with cruise ships, in for between-season refurbishment. When seen in company with the huge *Costa Classica* and the *Costa Allegra*, *Monterey*, *Mermoz*, *Delphin* and an Italian Railways ferry, the *Adriana* seemed a rather modest little ship.

But when built, she was quite significant. It was a time when the Greeks were developing their shipbuilding industry and the *Aquarius*, as she was then known, was one of the first sizeable passenger ships to come from a Greek yard. She may also have been the first cruise ship newly-built for Greek owners. Of course, these claims are always open to dispute – how do you define a cruise ship? Or for that matter, how do you define a Greek? (Were Home Lines, for instance, Greek, Italian or Panamanian?) However, in 1972 Hellenic Mediterranean Lines took delivery of this new cruise ship which they named *Aquarius*.

At that time Hellenic Mediterranean (or Elmes as they were often called) were, in the words of Laurence Dunn, 'among the aristocrats of the Greek passenger shipping business'. They can trace their origins back to the 1890s and were for many years the Yannoulatos family business. In the post-War years they ran a passenger/cargo service more or less the length of the Mediterranean, from Marseilles to the Levant, calling at Italian and Greek ports en route. They used smallish second-hand ships, but well enough refurbished and maintained to be able to compete with the vessels of the Adriatica and Turkish Maritime Lines. In 1960, with encouragement from the Greek government, they took delivery of a brand-new drive on/drive off car ferry, the *Egnatia*, which they placed in a joint service with Adriatica's similar *Appia* between Brindisi and Patras. Later with the introduction of the *Aquarius* in 1972, they entered the cruise market.

The new vessel was laid down as No. 54 at the United Shipping Yard Co. at Perama. She was launched on 15th September, 1971 and was later transferred to the new Kynosoura Dockyard on the Island of Salamis to be completed. Although she was entirely a passenger ship, without cargo holds, she was still given a decent length of bow – unlike some later small cruisers. Perhaps her most notable feature was the combined mast and smoke deflector which sprouted from the front of her funnel. She was powered by two V8-cylinder Pielstick diesel engines, built by the Chantiers de l'Atlantique at St. Nazaire. They were placed fairly far aft and reduction-geared to twin screws. There was a bulbous bow and two sets of stabilisers were fitted.

A fashionable Californian designer, Maurice Bailey, was brought in to plan much of the furnishing. A night club was included among the public rooms. Indeed, night-

**Notable when she came out in 1972 as one of the first purpose-built Greek cruise ships, the *Aquarius* was an elegant little ship with much more sheer than most of her contemporaries. She is here docked at Istanbul.** *Ambrose Greenway.*

**A notable meeting of cruise ships in the 'seventies. In the background are Karageorgis Lines' *Navarino* and Chandris' *Victoria*; in the foreground Hellenic Mediterranean's *Aquarius* and Kavounides' *Kentavros*.** *Laurence Dunn.*

life was one of the attractions of the ship. A brochure proclaimed 'the *Aquarius* at night is a bit like club-hopping in Europe' and catalogued the nocturnal activities in the lounges, bar, discotheque and the night-club – 'sleek steel and mauve velvet, filled with cozy couches, a curving staircase, stainless steel dance floor. There's nothing like it on the seas.' There were 136 cabins, mostly outside and all with private facilities and air-conditioning – things we take for granted to-day but which were still a matter for comment in the early '70s. The ship could accommodate up to 324 passengers, since in some of the cabins a third, Pullman berth could be let down, She was a smart, rather modernistic-looking ship and her funnel was painted in the Elmes colours – buff with a black top and a narrow blue band.

The *Aquarius* was built with a size and draught suitable for island-hopping cruises in the Aegean and also in the Caribbean. Completed by mid-June, 1972, she embarked on her first season of 7-day cruises out of Piraeus, including calls at Iraklion, Rhodes and other islands and Istanbul. Then, on 21st November she left Piraeus for Port Everglades, from where she began a series of 7- and 14-day cruises round the Caribbean marketed by the French Line. Unfortunately, on the 20th January, 1973 she reported the serious breakdown of her port engine. She managed to make her way on one engine to Cozumel island off the coast of Mexico but was eventually towed to Miami for repairs and was not back in action until the 17th February when she left Port Everglades on her return cruise to Piraeus via Cristobal, San Tomas de Castilla, San Juan and Las Palmas.

She did not return to the Caribbean for some years but continued her regular seasons of 7-day Aegean cruises from Piraeus, usually from April to November. The Winter of 1977-78 should have seen her running cruises out of Malaga to the Canaries, Morocco and Madeira under charter to a travel firm, but these were cancelled. However, the following Winter she re-appeared in the Caribbean, running 7-day cruises out of Nassau to Cap Haitien, San Juan, St. Thomas, and Puerto Plata. In subsequent Winters she was based variously at San Juan and Miami. For the rest of each year she maintained her regular Aegean schedule. There was talk that in 1984 she would run under charter to the newly-formed Ocean Cruise Line, but the deal fell through.

The hi-jacking of the Italian cruise ship *Achille Lauro* in October, 1985 and the murder of one of her passengers plunged the cruise industry in the Mediterranean into crisis. Potential passengers, understandably, shied away from the area. Several firms simply laid up their ships. Hellenic Mediterranean kept the *Aquarius* running throughout the Summer of 1986 but passenger bookings were disastrously low. Eventually the ship was impounded by a bank which held a mortgage on her. To add to the company's woes this resulted in the cancellation of a charter for some cruises in the Caribbean the following Winter. So desperate was the situation that the entire Hellenic Mediterranean fleet lay idle throughout the Summer of 1987. It was only the sale of the *Aquarius* and some other ships, including the modern ferry *Castalia*, which enabled the company to resume operations, concentrating almost entirely on the Brindisi – Patras ferry service.

The buyers of the *Aquarius*, in December, 1987, were a Liberian-registered company, Adriatic General Shipping Co. Ltd., who were said to have paid $7 million for her. The relationship between this concern and Jadrolinija, the state-owned Yugoslav company which we have already met in the chapter on the *Jedinstvo*, is not entirely clear but by mid-March the ship was being operated by the Yugoslavs under their country's own flag. She had been re-named *Adriana*. By 1992, with Yugoslavia now divided, she was flying the Croatian flag and ownership had passed to Jadrolinija themselves. They had long had strong links with German tour operators and it seems that for much of the time they operated the *Adriana* either block-booked or

Now Croatian-owned and called *Adriana*, the former *Aquarius* cruised widely in European waters in the 1990s. *Author's collection.*

under charter to German travel firms, including Seetours.

As the *Adriana*, the ship regularly spent Spring and early Summer in the Mediterranean, then moved to the Baltic for the High Season before returning to the Mediterranean for some final cruises in the late Summer and Autumn. She visited a much more diverse list of places than in her previous existence. Often starting from Venice, her Mediterranean ports of call ranged from Barcelona, Nice and Agadir to Ashdod and Istanbul. In 1991 she was one of the first cruise ships since the Second World War to call at the port of Durres in Albania, a country which had not hitherto welcomed foreign tourists. Her northern cruises, sometimes based at Bremerhaven or Cuxhaven, took her to the usual Baltic ports, including Tallinn where I saw her in 1994, and also occasionally up the Norwegian coast. While moving between the Mediterranean and the Baltic she sometimes called at British ports – Tilbury, Southampton, Kirkwall, Lerwick and, in 1996, the Pool of London. In the Summer of 1997, however, she was confined to the Mediterranean. Her size made her suitable for cultural cruises and Karawane, a well-known German firm specialising in this kind of tourism, was one of the travel companies who chartered her over the years.

When I saw her in Genoa in October, 1997, she had, it is now known, just been sold to a new French-owned company, Marina Cruises of Nice for $2 million. They registered her, still with the name *Adriana*, under the flag of St. Vincent and the Grenadines, but she still has Croatian officers. Among the work done on her during her stay at Genoa was the removal of the forward set of stabilisers. The intention has been to cater mainly for the French market, where, it has to be said, cruising has not caught on to anything like the same extent as in America, Britain or Germany. Marketed under the slogan Plein Cap, croisières de tradition française, she started her first cruise for her new owners on the 16th February, 1998, visiting Naples, Dubrovnik and Split and ending at Venice. Subsequent cruises, usually starting from Nice, have mainly taken her to various parts of the Mediterranean. There have, however, been other voyages, often under charter, which have visited more distant destinations. It was on one of these trips, that the *Adriana* lost a propeller at Helsinki in August, 1999 which resulted in the cancellation of a cruise.

The *Adriana* takes on the pilot near Funchal in November, 1996.
*Luís Filip Jardim.*

# 32

# Polarlys

### Polarlys

Completed, 1996. 11,341 gross tons. Length overall: 403 ft. 6¹/₂ ins. Breadth: 63 ft. 11¹/₂ ins. Draught: 16 ft. 1¹/₄ ins. Twin screw. Diesel. Service speed: 18 knots.

It was with more than just a twinge of disappointment that I learned from the sailing schedule that my overnight journey in October, 1996 on the Ålesund to Bergen leg of the Norwegian coastal express service would be aboard one of the new vessels rather than on one of the remaining traditional ships. In the event, I enjoyed my brief voyage on the almost brand-new *Polarlys* immensely and came away with a high regard for a ship which I had been told I should not like at all.

Times are changing on the Norwegian coast. The government subsidy which has kept the coastal express service (the Hurtigruten) going for more than a century seems likely to be withdrawn in 2001. The two companies which now run the service hope, however, to be able to continue the daily departures, year-round, from Bergen. The ships make an 11-day odyssey up the coast and back, serving 34 ports, with Kirkenes, way

beyond the North Cape and close to the border with Russia, as the turning point. In order to maintain this service the companies are trying to develop the tourist trade still further. Over the years, as the road network has improved and aeroplanes and fast ferries have taken some of the local traffic, tourist passengers have become increasingly important to the service. The original functions remain of maintaining a link with the remote and often tiny communities of the north; of carrying cargo, mail and local passengers; and, since 1982, of providing roll-on/roll-off facilities for motor vehicles – but it is

**The 11,300-ton *Polarlys* contrasts strongly with one of the last of the traditional Hurtigruten ships, the 2,500-ton *Lofoten*.** *Troms Fylkes and Ofotens og Vesteraalens DS..*

tourism and group travel which, it is hoped, will ensure the survival of the service. It has, after all, been advertised for years as 'The World's Most Beautiful Voyage' – a claim which owes very little to ad-man's hyperbole. So the new generation of 'coastal steamers' (although steam actually disappeared from the Hurtigruten in 1964) are much more akin to cruise ships than to the workhorses of years ago. They do still carry palletised cargo and provide a local service but the tourist passengers are much more insulated from it all. In the process the Hurtigruten is, no doubt, losing a little of its fascination but there is no denying that the new vessels are vastly more comfortable than their predecessors.

Over the years, certain Hurtigruten ships have become particular favourites. The *Erling Jarl* of 1949 was one, I am told. To-day, the darling of the fleet seems to be the *Lofoten* of 1964. She is a striking example of 'sixties streamlining and is said to be well-furnished and comfortable. My own previous experience of the Hurtigruten was a round trip in 1976 on the *Nordstjernen* of 1956 which seemed a somewhat plainly furnished ship, commanded by a stern captain. She was admirable,

**The interior decoration of the *Polarlys* is very much that of a modern cruise ship.** *Ulstein Verft..*

**A stamp celebrating the centenary of the establishment of the Hurtigruten in 1893.** *Author's collection.*

though, and she has survived. With age has come affection, particularly since she successfully revived the summer cruise service to Spitzbergen.

The six new ships introduced between 1993 and 1997 seem, at 400 feet and 11,000 tons, to dwarf the 1960s vessels of 280 feet and 2,500 tons and even make the middle generation of the early 1980s (350 feet and 6,000 tons) seem small. As we stood on the quay at Ålesund just before midnight watching the brisk approach of the brightly lit *Polarlys*, she did indeed seem a big ship – and even more so when, having tied up, she towered above us, for she is eight decks high. She looked every inch a cruise ship, with her superstructure spreading more or less the length of the hull and no sign of cargo gear. Freight was dealt with when a ramp in the side of the ship was cranked down hydraulically and a fork-lift truck trundled back and forth. The ramp is on the port side and is also used to give up to 50 cars (but no lorries) access to the vehicle deck. Bearing in mind the lessons of the *Estonia* disaster, that deck is subdivided. Much of the cargo space is refrigerated, fish being an important southbound freight.

From the passenger's point of view, the intimacy of the old Hurtigruten ships has been lost and, as Ted Scull pointed out after travelling on the *Kong Harald* in 1994, the new ships provide a much more indoor experience than the older ones. But in thirty years' time people will perhaps be feeling sentimental about the *Polarlys* and will bemoan the fact that 'they don't make ships like that any more'. She is, in fact, an extremely comfortable vessel. She and the other members of the new generation are, for instance, fitted with stabilisers which must be a long overdue boon on the more exposed passages of the route. The cabins, largely two-berth but with a few three-berth and also with six suites, are almost entirely outside and are surprisingly spacious and very pleasingly furnished. Indeed, there is a feeling of good quality about all the passenger quarters. Star-spangled ceilings and showy 'designer' décor may not please the traditionalists but, taken on her own terms, the *Polarlys* is a likeable ship. And here and there one finds small tributes to the past – half-models of the previous Hurtigruten ships which bore the name *Polarlys*; and pictures of deck and other scenes from the early years of the century when coastal travel really was pretty basic. In addition to the 474 passengers she can accommodate in her cabins and suites, the new *Polarlys* can carry a further 263 local port-to-port travellers. The facilities she provides include a restaurant, café, shop, observation lounges, bars, playroom, prison, saunas and conference rooms – but no casino and no swimming pool.

If the latest ships have brought a new sophistication to passenger travel on the Hurtigruten the *Polarlys* in particular is also a very sophisticated ship mechanically. She is driven by two 'father and son' units built by Ulstein Bergen. Each unit consists of two diesel engines of different sizes which together can provide a range of economical speeds; and each drives a controllable pitch propeller. Aft of the two propellers there is an additional thruster for use when the ship is moving slowly (or loitering, to use the rather suggestive technical term) or when she is manoeuvring, in which case the bow thrusters will also probably be brought into play. The *Polarlys* in fact, has a rather more complicated propulsion system than the other ships of the new generation. All six of them look fairly similar but there are, in fact, marked differences between them. The first three were built in Germany but the later ships have been products of Norwegian yards. *Polarlys* came from the Ulstein Verft's Hatlø dock. Ulstein have specialised in building offshore supply vessels and the *Polarlys* is not only one of the very few passenger ships they have produced but also the largest ship they have ever built. Construction started in February, 1995 and she was

floated out of her dock on the 8th December, 1995. The ceremonial naming took place on the 23rd March, 1996 and she was then handed over to her owners and took her place in the 11-ship fleet which maintains this historic service.

The *Polarlys* belongs to the Troms Fylkes Dampskibsselskap, one of the two concerns which these days operate the Hurtigruten. (The other one is the Ofotens og Vesteraalens Dampskibsselskab, more conveniently known as OVDS. This is a combination of two historic concerns, one of which, Vestersaalens, was the pioneer of the Hurtigruten. Very fittingly OVDS have called one of their new ships *Richard With* after the man who was responsible for starting the service.) The *Polarlys* and the other five new ships represent a massive act of faith in the future of the Hurtigruten and one wishes them, and their owners, well.

# Index